Anonymous

Passages in the lives of Helen Alexander and James Currie of

Pentland,

And other papers. Printed for family use, from original manuscripts and

papers in the possession of Francis Umpherston, Esq., Elmswood,

Loanhead. [With a genealogical table.]

Anonymous

Passages in the lives of Helen Alexander and James Currie of Pentland,
*And other papers. Printed for family use, from original manuscripts and papers in
the possession of Francis Umpherston, Esq., Elmswood, Loanhead. [With a
genealogical table.]*

ISBN/EAN: 9783337810924

Printed in Europe, USA, Canada, Australia, Japan

Cover: Foto ©ninafisch / pixelio.de

More available books at **www.hansebooks.com**

PASSAGES

IN THE LIVES OF

Helen Alexander and
James Currie,

OF PENTLAND.

And other Papers.

PRINTED FOR FAMILY USE,
FROM ORIGINAL MANUSCRIPTS AND PAPERS IN THE POSSESSION OF
FRANCIS UMPHERSTON, Esq., ELMSWOOD, LOANHEAD.

———

Belfast:
PRINTED BY MARCUS WARD & CO., ULSTER WORKS.
1869.

Prefatory Note.

——◦•◉•◦——

THESE *Memoirs of* ·Helen Alexander *and* James Currie *are printed verbatim from the original Manuscripts, with only a few alterations—not exceeding half-a-dozen—necessary to correct accidental mistakes of grammar. The account of* Helen Alexander *was written to her dictation in the beginning of* 1729, *shortly before her death; that of* James Currie *appears to have been written at an earlier date, as* Helen Alexander *refers to it in her narrative.*

There is in the possession of Mrs. Mathie *at* Dumbarton *a manuscript Memoir of* Helen Alexander. *Though substantially the same as that in the possession of* Mr. Umpherston, *it differs considerably in language, and is more overloaded with reflections and Scripture quotations. It bears internal evidence of having been written after* Helen Alexander's *death, and is most probably an enlarged version intended for the press.** *Nevertheless, I have preferred to print from the older copy, as being quainter, less encumbered with quotations, and containing the narrative as dictated by* Helen Alexander, *without the alterations made after her death.*

Helen Alexander's *imprisonment in the* Canongate Tolbooth *must have taken place between the* 11th June, 1683, *the date of* Andrew Gulon's *apprehension, and the end of that year. But I have not been able to find any notice of it or of her examination before the* Privy Council, *or any order for her release, in the* Privy Council Records, *which I have carefully examined from* August 1682 *to* October 1684.

The Letters from Sir Robert Hamilton *to* Helen Alexander *and* James Currie *are reprinted from* A collection of missive LETTERS written by the late Right Honourable Sir ROBERT HAMILTON to his

---

* *It has the following note, apparently in the handwriting of* James Currie :—

"I doe leave and lay upon JAMES UMPHERSTOUN and Mr. CHARLES UMPHERSTOUN to print this account with some letters from friends, and Mr. CHARLES to write a short preface. Likewise to cause print Sir ROBERT HAMILTON's letters to JAMES CURRIE corrected by WILLIAM McFORLING. Mr. CHARLES may review them : all done out of true love to the glorie of the Lord that ever came to sett His love upon the like of us."

Christian friends, *which forms part of a small book, published in* Edinburgh *in the year* 1762, *entitled* The CHRISTIAN'S CONDUCT: *or* A WITNESS for TRUTH against ERROR. *The Letters from* Mr. McMillan *and* Mr. Kid *are printed from manuscript copies in the possession of* Mrs. Mathie.

The first monument in the Greyfriar's Churchyard *to the memory of the Martyrs was erected by* James Currie *and others in* 1706, *and, as stated by* Mr. James Brown, *in his work, entitled* The Epitaphs and Monumental Inscriptions in Greyfriar's Churchyard, Edinburgh, *consisted only of an open Bible, with a quotation from the Revelation. This stone was preserved, and forms the under part of the monument renewed in* 1771. *The petition presented to the* Town Council *in* 1706, *for permission to erect the monument, has not been preserved among the Council Records, so that the names of those who assisted* James Currie *in the work are probably irrecoverably lost. The following order, however, was passed on the petition :—*

EDINR. 28 AUGUST 1706.

WEDNESDAY. THE WHICH DAY anent the memoriall given in to the Councill representing that there was a monument prepared to be erected near the place of interment of those persons who suffered in the late times and were buried in the Grayfrier

Churchyaird and that at the charges of private hands : and therfore craveing that the Councill would allow the said monument to be put up w'out paying of anything to the Kirk theasurer as was done at Glasgow and other places of the natione there being noe Inscriptione to be put upon the tomb but the 6 chapter of the revelatione verse 9 : 10 and 11 : which being considered be the Councill they granted the desire therof and allowed the said monument to be put up accordingly at the sight of the Dean of Gild : WHERANENT thir presents shall be a warrand.

C. U. A.

Edinburgh,
March 31, 1869.

PASSAGES

IN THE LIFE OF

Helen Alexander.

An Account of the Lord's dealings with HELEN ALEXANDER, *Spouse first to* CHARLES UMPHERSTON, *tenant in* PENTLAND ; *and then Spouse to* JAMES CURRIE, *merchant in* PENTLAND, *for the which he blefses the Lord that provided him such a Spouse, who lived together religiously for the space of forty-two years, and was removed by death into* HEAVEN *on the* 10th OF MARCH, 1729 ; *who dyed as fhe had lived, giving her laft* TESTIMONY *againft all the courfes of the present time, giving evident by her laft words of her tender heart being broken for the fins of Church and State, and her* TESTIMONY *againft both.*

I—LIVING in the course of the world with others (although praifes to the Lord who keeped me from the common pollutions that youth is polluted with), and having my own difficultys in my father's house, 1676.—About he marrying another wife after my mother dyed, which 53 years ago. proved very hard to me—went and dwelt with my fifter for some time in the Parifh of *Dirltoun,* my lot being in

B

that Pariſh and in the Pariſh of *Lintoun*, where I was born and brought up till the aforesaid time that my father was married. In these Pariſhes there were no Curates at that time.

And when I was firſt married, I was at the age of eighteen years ; and having my lot caſten in this place (*Pentland*), where there were several godly persons who were going to hear the persecuted Ministers about *Edinburgh* and the *Good-trees*, the Lord inclined my heart to go with them, and I went with them where I did hear *Mr. Welch, Mr. Donald Cargil,* and several others, where the Lord bleſsed their preaching to my soul, yet not thoroughly convinced of the evill of hearing the Prelaticall Curates: for I thought if these good people went to the Curates, I would go too. [So far ſhould we be from following any but in so far as they follow the Lord.]

But one time I was going to the *Good-trees* the reſt of the people were away to *Edinburgh*, and I returned home again with a sore heart. And I sate down by the way at a dyke and took my Bible, and the Lord brought that place of Scripture in *Isaiah* xli. 17 :— *When the poor and needy seek water, and there is none, and their tongue faileth for thirſt, I the Lord will hear them, I the God of* ISRAEL *will not forsake them.* Ver. 18. *I will open the rivers in high places, and fountains in the midſt of the valleys ; I will make the wilderneſs a pool of water, and the dry land springs of water.* Ver. 19. *I will plant in the wilderneſs,* and so forth. But after that, I was at a communion at *Ormistoun,* where I did hear *Mr. David Williamson* upon that in *Isaiah* lxvi. 2 :—*For all those things hath mine hand made, and all those things have been, saith the Lord:* which was a pleasant sermon to my soul.

And afterwards I was in the *Eaſt Country* seeing my ſister ; and I had spoken some worldly discourse upon the Lord's Day ; and for that ſin and other ſins the Lord awakened my conscience, and convinced me throughly what I was by nature, and the evill of hearing the perjured curates, although they ſhould have taken my life, which was my tryall afterwards. O what a fearful fight got I of myself! that I thought there was none upon the earth like me, and wondered that I was out of *Hell;* and I thought I saw the flames of *Hell,* and wondered that the earth did not open its mouth and swallow me up ; for I thought I did nothing but fin. O what soul-trouble I was under ; for I thought it was need-lefs for me to pray, for all my duties were defiled with fin. But as if it had been said from the Lord, *Mint, and be doing;* for I pafst the sentence of condemnation againft myself. And at that time it might have been seen what a weary creature I was ; which was seen in my countenance. And at one time, looking up to *Heaven,* I thought they were well that did go there, but I will not win there ; but I was glad how many did go there. But as if it had been spoken to me from the Lord, *Thou fhalt have thy part and portion there;* and then how chearfull was I for some time. And I found the Lord was present with me where I was praying, and then, through the Lord's goodnefs, I found a great weight taken off me ; but O, how sweet a time had I then. But after-wards, falling secure, and not being so tender as I fhould have been, I fell in great fears and doubts, and thought all was delu-fion, untill the Lord directed me, and I was directed. So I cryed to the Lord that He would reveal to me by His Word and Spirit ; and it was revealed to me—that sweet Scripture, never to be for-gotten by me, *Jeremiah* xxxi. 3 :—*The Lord hath appeared to me of old, saying, Yea, I have loved thee with an everlafting love; there-fore with lovingkindnefs have I drawn thee.*

So in all my straits I had recourse to the Lord's blefsed Word, according to that sweet Scripture, *Psalm* cxix. 50 :—*For in my straits I am revived by this Thy Word alone; it is my comfort in my afflidion.* O what of the Lord had I then ! and many a sweet smile had I of His fair countenance for a confiderable time ; as it is in *Isaiah* lxvi. 12, 13 :—*For thus saith the Lord, Behold, I will extend peace to her like a river, and the glory like a flowing ftream :*

then fliall ye suck, ye fliall be borne upon her fides, and dandled upon her knees, &c. And many a sweet blink had I of His countenance, and all my bands were loosed.

1678. But alas I gave the Lord an ill requitall. For at that time the *Highland Hoft* came to the *Weft* to opprefs, and the Tenants were to put out their Militia in this country; and my firft husband sent for the key of the cheft where the filver was, to give out some money to the Militia men that were going to opprefs the honeft people and the honeft cause. And I was convinced of the evill of it from that of *Obadiah*, from the 10th to the 15th verfe :—*For thy violence againft thy brother* JACOB *fliame fliall cover thee,* &c. ; for I thought the giving of the key was an afsenting to the thing. And after I did that, O how did the Lord frown and hide His sweet face from me. O what a terror it was to me when the Lord awakened my conscience. This I say, because even there many that profefsed religion gave out that money, which was finfull. But O how clear it was to me ; though they would have said :— *What needs you be troubled; wherefore may not ye pay it as well as other profefsors ?* But that was no salve to my confcience.

1679. But then at the breach of *Bothwell,* how was I con- cerned with them, and went and met them a mile *Weft* from *Edinburgh.* They were faid to be 1200 of them. O how grieved was I to see them ; their cloathes being taken from them, and being brought in half-naked—some only their fhirts, some mutches on their heads—to the *Greyfreer's Yard;* and of that number there were fourfcore wounded put in *Heriot's Work.* And I did gather some money and fhirts of my own, and took in to them.

And then I had a fore tryall of my husband's death ; which was a sore tryall to me. I had likewife a fharp tryall afterward ; for, being at a preaching in the *Yearn Craig,* one *James Porteous, Eaftfide,* tenant there, went to the *Laird* of *Pentland* and told him ; who held a *Court,* and I was the firft that was inquired at if I was at the preaching. And they said, "Ye muſt either confeſs or deny;" and I said, "I will not deny; for Chriſt hath said, *He that denyeth Me before men, him will I deny before My Father which is in Heaven.*" And, alas, to my grief, severals denyed that were there.

And afterward, *Skeen* of *Hallyard* held a *Court*, and fined me of 50 *lib.* Scots; but I did not compear at his *Court;* for I thought it not right to compear at their *Courts.* And afterward I was more hardly put at, that I was forced either to go to the *Kirk* and hear the perjured Curates, or otherwise to quite the Room and go from it; which I was willing to do rather than to go to hear the Epiſcopall Curates and forſake Chriſt and His way. And many said to me I was a fool for quitting of such a good Room. And I was so helped of the Lord to make a right choice that, though it had been covered with gold, I would rather quite it than quite with my sweet Lord, Jeſus Chriſt. For the Lord did uphold me with the right hand of His righteousneſs, and so I did accordingly quite it upon these terms, though I had three fatherleſs young children then ; but O then the Word of the Lord was sweet to me in those trying times.

And then another tryall I had. In case that the enemies had come and taken all that we had, I made a diſpoſition to *Robert Umpherſton*, my brother-in-law, and went and delivered all to him that was about the house—horse, moult, and corn, and all. Then I thought I have nothing now ; but then that sweet word came into my mind—*Prov.* xviii. 10 :—*The name of the Lord is a ſtrong tower, and the righteous flee into it and are safe.* And I thought what we had would not maintain us in meat and cloathing ; and then that sweet word came into my mind—*Matt.* vi. 26 :—*Behold the fowls of the air: for they sow not, neither do they reap, nor gather into barns ; yet your heavenly Father feedeth them. Are ye not much better than they ?* Ver. 28. *And why take ye thought for raiment ? Conſider the lilies of the field, how they grow: they toil not, neither do they spin:* ver. 29. *Yet I say unto you, Solomon in all his glory was not arrayed like one of these.* And after these Scriptures were borne in upon my mind, I durſt not doubt of God's providence; and so we were well provided for all our dayes, in meat and cloaths; and my children likewise. But at that time I was forced to leave my house, and durſt not ſtay at home for fear of being apprehended. But I cannot tell how good and kind the Lord was to me, and saved me from many ſinfull snares that others fell into; for I never thought it right to give anything to any of those that were enemies to my dear Lord, either fines or Militia money, which I did allways testify againſt.

And about the year 1682, *Andrew Gulon,* who was execute, did sometimes come to my house; for I allways thought it my duty to harbour any of the Godly, and if I thought they were Godly, though they differed in judgment, yet I willingly entertained them, but especially those that were ſtraighteſt in their judgment, and those who were most perſecute for righteousneſs' sake. And when the Lord diſcovered to me the evill of the *Indulgence* and *Indemnity,* I did allways teſtify againſt it. And those whom the Lord honoured to suffer cleanly those I did esteem most.

And so, he being taken, it was thought that *Mr. M'Naught,* the Curate, had informed againſt me to the *Councill;* and the *Councill* put it to the *Laird* to apprehend me, who then was *Sir Alexander Gibson* (little to his credite). When I had been out of mine own house for several days and weeks, he came one morning with his son, *Mr. Alexander Gibson* (who fell off his horse, and did break his neck, *March 3rd,* 1729), and his servants, when I was ſitten down to go about family worſhip and sung a part of a *Psalm.* And I eſsayed to make my eſcape beneath a bed; but they lighted a candle and found me, and brought me to a house. And he advised me to go to the *Kirk,* and I said to him I would rather beg my bread with my children or I took any ſinfull way. And I said to him that I ſhould go out of the town and off his ground, and then he may say I was not on his ground ; and he said that would ruin his family. I anfwered again that way that he was taking was the ready way to ruin him and his family both. So they took me away to the *Abbey.* One *Alexander Broun,* a servant in *Pentland,* was one of them who were my guard by the way ; and so, within a fhort time after, he fell fick, and in his ficknefs he was (in the Lord's righteous judgment) smitten with vermin ; and I went to see him, and the woman said unto me, *Hold out bye, goodwife; for he is creeping with lice.* And the other who guarded me was one *John Logan, Smith* and *Officer* in *Pentland,* who or he dyed I went to see him. And his wife said to me, *He is rotting away in his own filth ;* and, as if he had been a beaft, was carrying away his filth for that and his other wickednefs venting againft the people of God.

And when I was carried to the *Abbey,* the souldiers took me into a house, and when in the house, I having my Bible with me, every place of Scripture I looked upon was sweet to me, especially that in *Rev.* vi. 9, 10, 11 :—*And when he had opened the fifth seal, I saw under the altar the souls of them that were flain for the Word of God, and for the teftimony which they held : and they cryed with a loud voice, saying, How long, O Lord, holy and true, doft Thou not judge and avainge our blood on them that dwell on the earth ? And white robes were given unto every one of them, that they fhould rest yet for a little season,* &c. *Rev.* vii. 13, 14, 15 :— *And one of the Elders answered, saying unto me, What are these which are arrayed in white robes? . . . And he said to me, These are they which came out of great tribulation, and have wafhed their robes and made them white in the blood of the Lamb. Therefore are they before the throne of God,* &c. *Psalm* l. 15 :—*Call upon Me in the day of trouble : I will deliver thee, and thou fhalt glorify Me. Psalm* lv. 22 :—*Caft thy burden on the Lord, and He fhall suftain thee,* &c. And many other places of Scripture were made sweet to me in the time.

And one of the men said, *Ye have the* CHANCELLOUR *and other great men to go before;* and I answered and said, *I have a greater Judge to go before, the Judge of all the Earth.* And then there cometh a party of souldiers, and took me to prison. I bleſs the Lord all fear was taken away from me. O how sweet and kind was the Lord to me, and made good His Word to me, *I will be with you in trouble to deliver you,* &c. But that which was soreſt to me—I was brought down from the room where I was, and put in the room where were *John Gib,* and *Jameson,* and one *Sanders Monteith,* and *Ann Stewart,* all vile and abominable blasphemers. That woman would have sewed her seams and wrought on the Lord's day, and when we were praying, and ſinging, and reading, they did interrupt us. O what grief of heart it was to me to hear and see their blasphemy. They would have said they knew of no *Heaven* or *Hell,* nor no God. And how beaſtly they were in lying with one another. And I thought or I had been another Sabbath in their company I would rather chosen to go to a gibbet; for this their carriage to me was like death. But to His name be all the praise who delivered me.

When I had been some days in prison, I was brought down from the prison to the *Abbey* by a guard of souldiers to the *Chancellour* and *Biſhop Patterson.* O what a pleasant while I had at that time going down the ſtreet with the guards. And when I was brought before the *Chancellour,* who was Preſident, and *Biſhop Patterson,* I was interrogate by *Sir William Patterson* if I went to the *Kirk.* I said I would not go to the *Kirk* though they ſhould take my life from me. They queſtioned me if *Andrew Gulon* came to my house, and I said, He did. He aſked me why I gave him cloath to work; I answered, He was honeſt. He aſked if any vagabonds came to my house, and I said, No; (for so they termed these sufferers.) But the above *Sir William Patterson* aſked if the *Biſhop's* death were murder, and if the *King's* authority was lawfull. I answered they ſhould not aſk these things at women. But O how kind was the Lord to me; and all fear was taken away when I was before them. So I was returned to prison again; however, I was delivered from these lyons; for the Lord (glory to His name) brought me out without the leaſt complyance (after 11 weeks' imprisonment), either by bonding or anywise yielding; for I would . . . . nor did I own them in anything, nor did I consent to pay the jeoler's fee, or anything that might imply any complyance. So the Lord delivered me—praise to His wonder-working Providence for me, when many tall cedars (to whom in my eyes I seemed a small ſhrub) were left to comply, and some seeming eminent were left by God that they took the *Test*. There were 32 prisoners took it the time I was in prison. O what grief of heart it was to me to see and hear them so far left by God.

1683. And when I came home behind my brother, I asked him, *How am I won out of prison?* He said, *Had ye been brought again before them it might coſt you your life.* However, the Lord brought me home to my three children, who were fatherleſs three years before I was taken (which children were well provided for afterward; praise to the Lord for it). But before I came out they said I was to dye; and I aſked who said that, and they said all that were in the prison said it. And so I was resolved to dye, and sent home word to provide and make ready my winding-ſheet; for, through the ſtrength of the Lord, I was resolved to lay down my life rather than comply either with the Prelaticall Curates, or any other course of complyance, or to own the authority of the Tyrant who was then upon the throne. There is one thing to be noticed, that, when the word came home that I was to dye, how concerned were friends that were at home; for one said, *If ſhe dye, I ſhall never work any more, either to spin or card;* and one other friend said ſhe would go out of her wit, so concerned were they about my death. But now the Lord brought me home, to the praise of the Lord's goodneſs, who hath hitherto

c

preserved me from many evills of sin or complyance that many, as I thought were far better than me, did fall into.

And when I came home my friends were angrie that I harboured any of the persecuted people of the Lord, and said I would bring myself into trouble again. Then I thought, what cared I for a house, and wherefore have I a house if it be not to intertain the people of the Lord ; which I allways willingly did. For *Mr. James Renwick* came home that same year an ordained miniſter. I scrupled to hear him at the firſt, because they said he was ordained by those who had the organs, till I was better informed by himself; and the account of his life and death gives a full account. And then friends about *Pentland* and *Edinburgh* brought him out to *Woodhouselee* old house, and I went and heard him ; and after that I intertained him and those who did accompany him, and I thought it my duty upon all hazard. And many a time he came to my house after that. Though the persecution grew very hot after he came home untill he was taken, I went in all hazard to the fields and heard him.

Then some years after, that wofull *Tolleration* came out, which made my heart grieved; and wo was I when the Presbyterian Ministers imbraced it; for I thought none but the Prelaticall party should imbrace it. And here I leave my *Teſtimony* against it, both now and formerly, and againſt all the ſteps of defeċtion. The Lord left them then that they never recovered again to what they were before *Bothwell*.

And when *Mr. James Renwick* was in my house, he was telling how he and those with him were afsaulted by the *Lord Hindfoord* and the Militia men about *Dunsire Common*, and they all put on their arms and were resolved to fight. And it was said to *Mr. Renwick* that they might make their teſtament; he answered, *We made it oftener nor once in the day.* This was in my hearing.

And about this time I might not be seen in my own house, nor in the town. And being *West* seeing my father at *Lintoun*, I came home with the fever on me ; and when I came to my own house there was a woman in the house spinning ; and fearing fhe had put me out and discovered me, there was one stood up till I went by ; and when I went to my bed I was all trembling for cold, for I durſt not go to the fire for fear of the woman, and so my daughter came ben the house and lay down to keep me warm. And I had a long fever; but my Lord, that many a time brought me through, brought me through at this time, for which I blefs the Lord. It was for His sake I suffered that and many other things ; but my soul hath cause to blefs the Lord that He was aye with me in all my tryalls.

About this time, 1683, *Mr. James Renwick* came home ordained from *Holland;* and *Mr. John Flint* came home thereafter, whom I never thought it my duty to hear, because he was not lawfully ordained : he had only a teſtimony of his learning. And I had many debeates with them that were for him. And the worthy *Mr. James Renwick* and those with him gave *Teſtimony* against *Mr. John Flint*, which *Teſtimony* I adhere to, and to all the honeſt *Teſtimonys* that have been given by those who keeped the Lord's way. And I was allways against extreams on both hands, for the Lord guided me ; and I had allways a sympathy with those who were in diſtrefs ; for when the prisoners were sent to *Dunottar Caſtle*, I did gather some money and some fhirts and gave to them who needed them, as I did many a time when they were in prison.

1687. And so being married in the year 1687, *Nov.* 30, by the worthy *Mr. James Renwick*, I thought my end in marrying was that we might have religious discourse when we were awake in our beds.

And when *Mr. Renwick* was execute, I went and saw him in prison ; and I said to him, *Ye will get the white robes;* and he said, *And palms in my hands.* And when he was execute, I went in to the *Greyfreer's Yard*, and I took him in my arms till his cloathes were taken off, and I helped to wind him before he was put in the coffin.

And another tryall I had after my marriage was—one *Captain Justice* * came to apprehend my Husband ; but he, being not at home, escaped. About the time before *Mr. Renwick* was taken, there were in *Pentland* about 9 or 10 bairns, none of them above 14 years of age, mett together for prayer.† And the Lord helped me to be very usefull among them, and I did encourage them, for which they had respect to me to my dying day. Likewise I was hearing *Mr. David Houſton* in *Lammer-muir*, where I heard him say, *We will be quite of Popery and Prelacy, but that wofull thing* ERASTIANISM *will be your greateſt tryall;* which is proven a sad truth.

1687.

But now what I underwent in my married life, viz., the sore trouble of my children's death, especially my sons *Thomas* and *James*, whose elegy is extant ; and far more, what the Lord brought me through in the six times cutting of my dear child, *Robert Ebenezer*, for so he was defigned to be called. And how sore his not being baptized was to me. At that time there was none that we could with freedom receive that benefite from. But I thought if it were to have carryed him upon my back an hundred miles, I would gladly have done it, if we could have gotten those that were not involved in the wofull *Tolleration* and *Indulgences* (and they made no true acknowledgment of it), and other sinfull courses. I remember (among many sweet Scriptures that were brought to my mind) one Scripture, as I was defiring of the Lord that he might glorify His name in the carrying through of my child so frequently cutt, and it was that in *John* xvii. :—*I have glorifyed My name, and I will glorify it again*—with many others as before ; for in all my troubles and straits I had aye recourse to the sweet Scriptures.

* Justice was the officer who apprehended James Renwick.
† See APPENDIX, Note A, *The Children's Covenant.*

And likewise the *Oath* of *Allegiance* and the *Oath* of *Abjuration* and the wofull *Union*—my soul was grieved with these courses, and I thought no Presbyterian Minister could have complyed with them; which courses with many others (especially since the year 1679) I leave my *Teſtimony* againſt; and I leave my *Teſtimony* to all the honeſt *Teſtimonys* before and ſince, even to this year, viz. 1729.

There are many paſsages of my life, if they had been carefully noticed and written in the time; but my Husband hath written the paſsages of what the Lord (glory to His name) did for him and me in our married ſtate—near to 80 paſsages which are upon record. As it is in *Psalm* cvii. 43 :—*Whoso is wise and will obſerve these things, even they ſhall undcrſtand the loving-kindnefs of the Lord.* But now to the riches of God's grace that when the Lord brought my children to the conception in my womb of their having life and a living soul, I devoted them to the Lord, and gave them away to the Lord, according to that word, *I will be a God to you and to your seed;* which the Lord graciously made out; for my young children that were taken away by death had the evidences of grace in them when alive. And likewise I sought it from the Lord to my children that ſurvived that they might get good and goodly wives and my daughter to get a godly husband, which, to the commendation of the Lord's wonderfull Providence, He did so provide for them: which, I think, parents ſhould ſincerely seek from God.

Her ordinary when ſhe sang the Lord's praise, either in fellowſhip or in the family, was the 105th Psalm, *which was the laſt* Psalm *ſhe sang; sometimes the 63rd and 72nd and 84th for ordinary, and ſhe had these* Psalms *by heart, and the whole* Catechism *by tongue.*

An Account

OF

THE MANNER IN WHICH *HELEN ALEXANDER* WAS LIBERATED FROM PRISON.

Written from FAMILY TRADITION *by her Great-Grandson,*
CHARLES UMPHERSTON.

———•—•—•———

HE manner of her getting out of prifon was as followeth: — She was a Tenant of *Sir Alexander Gibson's.* According to the tyranny of the times he was liable to a fine if he allowed any person to remain on his ground that entertained any of the persecuted party, or did not hear the Curates. Both of these supposed crimes she was guilty of. *Sir Alexander* took her prifoner to *Edinburgh.* After doing this he could get no reft in his mind, and would do anything in his power to get her set at liberty. After fhe was some time in prifon, being afraid fhe would lose her life, he forged a petition in her name, in which fhe was said to comply with the *Test,* or what would procure her liberty. *Sir Alexander* made his forgery known to some of the *Council,* who agreed with him in prefenting it. When it was presented, one of those who were ignorant of its being forged said the prifoner fhould be brought to the bar, and see if fhe acknowledged it. Those of *Sir Alexander's* party said there was no need, for that there was no doubt fhe would acknowledge it. Without much being said about it, the petition was granted and an order sent to liberate her.

—⋙⟐⟐⋘—

PASSAGES

James Currie.

These are some remarkable passages in my life, to the commendation of the Lord's love and kindness to me: and this as my lairge TESTIMONY *; I have one shorter. I send this to* WILLIAM M'NEILL.

FTER the example of the people of the Lord in Scripture, who did rehearse what the Lord had done for them, as *Abraham, Isaac,* and *Jacob*: as (from *Gen.,* chap. xii. to xxv.) all the way the Lord led *Abraham,* and tryed him by famine and hazard of his life, and by trying him to offer his only son *Isaac;* and (from that to chap. xxviii.) what the Lord did for *Isaac;* and from the xxviii. to the l. chap. there is a rehearsall of God's gracious benefites to *Jacob,* his serving of *Laban* 21 years, how he endured and how the Lord brought him through many difficultys ; and likewife his son *Joseph,* what he endured. I say it was the practice of the Lord's people to remember all the way the Lord led them : and how carefull they were to speak to the commendation of God's goodnefs. And according to that Scripture, *Deut.* viii. 2 :—*And thou shalt remember all the way that the Lord thy God led thee these forty years in the wildernefs, to humble thee and to prove thee, to know what was in thine heart, whether thou wouldest keep His commandments or not.* Ver. 3. *And He humbled thee and suffered thee to hunger,* &c. Ver. 18. *But thou shalt remember the Lord thy God, for it is He that giveth thee power to get wealth,* &c. Likewise what *David,* the Servant of the Lord came through; what he endured from wicked *Saul,* what he suffered by him and other wicked men, as *Ahitophel,* yea, and by his own son *Absalom*; and what difficulties he came through, the first and fecond books of *Samuel,* and the book of *Psalms* give account. What troubles and difficulties, what ſtraits, he met with when his own men spoke of ſtoning him, and being forced to flee out of *Jerusalem* for his own son; how humble he is brought :— *If he say he hath delight in me,* &c. : *Let* SHEMEY *curse, it may be the Lord hath bidden him.* So I say we see how this is recorded, and likewise we see what the great Apostle rehearseth, what great deliverances he met with, as in the book of the *Acts,* and 2 *Cor.,* chap. xi, from verse 23 to the end.

Wherefore, according to the Lord's command in Scripture, and the practice of the Lord's people both of old and of late, I have designed, and through the Lord's ſtrength and grace afsisting me, resolved (as the Lord will help), fingly to give some account of some remarkable deliverances from my youth; but more especially from the time the Lord, in His infinite love, took a gracious dealing with me, that it may be ſtrengthening to me in new ſtraits; and likewise this may witnefs against me if I shall forsake the Lord after so many deliverances, and the Lord's gracious dealing with me. And that this may be a *Testimony* to the Lord's noble cause and controverted truth (if there be no other left by me), and likewise of the Lord's gracious dealing with me (according to that *Psalm—Come and I will tell you what the Lord hath done for my soul),* and what the Lord did for me and my family, and my child *Robert Ebenezer*, for so I may call him, for hitherto the Lord helped him—I say, what the Lord did for us in the day of our ſtraits, and heard our prayers and gave a wonderfull deliverance. So I have defigned to give some account of the speciall mercies and deliverances that I remember from my birth (being born in the year 1656); but more particularly from the time that the Lord took a dealing with me by the preaching of some persecuted ministers, about the year 1674, being then about eighteen years old; likewise to give some account of the back-ſliding courfes of this time, that I know from my sad experience, and was witnefs to the moſt part of it with a sad heart; by what degrees and ſteps the poor people in this land were carryed away with the miniſters, which I expect there will be a faithfull account of, as there is somewhat of them in the *Proteſtation againſt the Tolleration, Hind let loose,* and the *Informatory Vindication.*

1st. Remark.—The firſt remarkable deliverance that I remember of was, when going through a water, the water, being great, took me down a great way; yet the Lord preserved me and brought me safe through.

2nd Rem.—The second remark of God's kyndnefs was, when at School I took some hatred at banning and swearing, so that I said to the reſt of my school-fellows, *Tell the Maſter if you hear me swear.*

3rd Rem.—When I was at School at the time that the Western men were beat, in the year 1666, I thought, *O, if I were like these men that mere executed;* and I had a great liking to them, though I could not give a reason.

4th Rem.—After that I grew ill, and would bann and swear, and would have angred my mother, my father being dead (he died in the year 1672). One time I had angred my mother, and there was a horse at the door which did bite me, which I observed at the time, it was for angring of my mother.

5th Rem.—I was put to a trade in the Pariſh of *Tranent,* and

D

heard the Curates there for more than two years; but got no good of them. I was very proud and vain, and grew very ill under these hirelings' miniſtry.

6th Rem.—But it pleased the Lord not to let me go on in the ſinfull course of hearing them; for one Sabbath morning I was thinking to go to hear the Curates, and sometimes thinking to go to hear a Presbyterian Miniſter; at length the Lord determined my heart to go to the Presbyterian Miniſter; and after that I never heard a Curate but with reluctance.

7th Rem.—I being not well acquaint, yet following on from *Ormiston Kirk*, not then knowing the difference between the Indulged and others that were outted ministers who were persecuted, went, after the preaching was done, from *Ormiston Kirk* to *Pencaitland Wood*, where *Mr. David Williamson* dwelt; and I heard him at his own house, where the Lord made His own word succeſsfull as to conviction, that I took some conviction of the evill of my wayes (but was seeking something in myself, and of my own righteousneſs), and was convinced of the evill of hearing the Curates; yet I fear and think till afterwards, the work of converſion was not wrought.

8th Rem.—After this I was resolving to go *East* from that place about 20 miles, to have wrought with a friend; but I took such a vehement pain in my leggs that I was not able to go, but was forced to return home to my mother's house in the *Temple* Pariſh, where the Lord helped me to be usefull in employing me afterwards to fetch out Miniſters to the fields in that country ſide.

9th Rem.—After I returned and set about my employment— which was a fearfull and ſinfull thing, what through fear and what through shame, diſenters being so few (as they were called *Puritants* and *Whigs*) in that Pariſh, there being only three or four that withdrew from the Curates' *Kirks;* and I thought my friends would not own nor countenance me, therefore—flesh and blood prevailed that I went and heard one Curate called *Traint* (who

was much for *Prelacy*), though for two years before I had not
heard them. So I went, as I remember, fix or seven Sabbaths;
but the Lord (glory to His great name) would not let me ftay in the
tents of thefe wicked men. For at that time I fell so away that
I could scarce pray a word, either alone or with others; for I went
over the belly of light and knowledge. It is true when the Lord
was convincing me of the evill of it, the last Sabbath I heard him,
it was a terror to me to hear him speak of the name of God when
he was preaching, for I thought it was a taking of the name of
God in vain. So little were his words bleft, that they were
blafted; and, as I said, I was so far left of the Lord under
his miniftry, that I would have banned and sworn. But the Lord
in His gracious love and free grace, would not leave me there.
Falling on that Scripture, *Luke* xiii. 6, 7, 8, where our Lord came
to the fig-tree these three years and found no fruit on it, and bade
Cut it down; why cumbereth it the ground? and another place,
Matt. xxi. 19, *Let never fruit grow on thee any more.* Now I
thought I was the barren fig-tree; for I had been profefsing near
three years; and reading the book called *The false Profefsor tryed
and cast*, I thought I was the very perfon. But O, the wonderful
love of God manifefted in Jesus Chrift, that did not leave me; for
as I was reading about the fig-tree, I was caft into such fearfull
horror and terror of conscience, that for some nights and dayes I
fleeped little or none. But while I was lying on my bed my
loynes would have shaken, and my knees smitten one againft
another; and I thought I was like *Cain* and *Judas*; and that
Scripture in *Isaiah* viii. 22:—*They shall look upon the earth and
behold dimnefs and anguifh.* Then *Satan*, that loves to fish in
muddy waters, was not wanting in his temptations; all things then
were a burden to me: and the Lord so far humbled me that I
thought the poor beggars happy; for when I had seen them I
would have thought, that body may get *Heaven*, but I will not
get *Heaven*.

10*th Rem.*—When I was toffing up and down, and to and fro, thinking allways I was the barren fig-tree ; and for going to hear the perjured Prelaticall Curates, which was the cause of the Lord's leaving me to the former evills I was guilty of—at this time, as I said before, the Lord (in His wonderfull gracious love, who will not break the bruised reed nor quench the smoking flax) did, for holy and wise ends, drive me out of myself, and did let me see the evill of fin which I had not seen before : I say, the dreadfull evill of fin I had not seen, and how dishonouring it is to God, and how I had grieved the Holy Spirit, and, like *Judas*, betrayed the Lord Jesus. The Lord did, as it were, hold me over the brink of *Hell*, and did let me see there was nothing but as it were an hair-breadth to keep me from it but the Lord, who I hope wrought that good work of converfion. For I then saw that which I had not seen before : I saw myself loft, and by nature a child of wrath, and that I was undone without a noble Redeemer ; for till then I was seeking to win to *Heaven* by the *Covenant* of *Works* for three years time. So, to the praise of His wonderfull free grace and free love, I was alone in the corner of a house in *Nicolson*, when I saw, as it were, the Lord Jesus ftanding before me, so that I never had gotten such a fight of Him before; and that never-to-be-forgotten Scripture, *Psalm* lxxxix, from the 30th to the 35th verses, but especially that word, 33rd verse, *I will not take my love from him*, I have found to my experience. And rising from my knees, with a chearfull coun-tenance, with that word, *I will not take my love from you*, I was no more sad for near the space of a year after. I had a sweet time then in the world ; and I may say it was there I firft caft my anchor, and have found the Lord faithfull, which I reserve to mention afterwards when I come to it.

11*th Rem.*—At this time, after the Lord recovered me, and as I hope beftowed His speciall grace upon me, O then how was I concerned with others, both with their souls and bodys ; for, as I was helped, I gave willingly to the poor. But O how did I bewail and was troubled for the poor people that were going to hear the Curates ; for I thought their souls were perifhing, and I was ſtill persuading all that would be persuaded to forbear hearing of them (there being only four or five that diſsented). And I pitied them greatly that would go to hear them ; for I thought if they had felt the anger of God as I had done, they would not go hear these soul-murderers.

12*th Rem.*—I, going to hear *Mr. Thomas Patterson* at *Borthwick*, was edified by him, not knowing the difference. I had occasion to hear *Mr. Robert Trail*, who preached after the *Kirk* scailled, viz., at *Borthwick;* and heard him with much satisfaction for a time till he would not preach except all the people were within doors. However, for the space of ten or twelve Sabbaths I had a sweet time of it, the Lord wonderfully bleſſing His Word both to my soul and to my memory—as some texts of Scripture in *Ezekiel* xii. and others. By this time, from the four or five formerly mentioned, they came to eighteen that did forbear hearing of the Curates, at which I was glad. And at this time (which is not to be omitted), it being in the winter, and being late at night or we scailled, there was a ſtar that gave us a great light from the *Weſt* in the home-going.

13*th Rem.*—At this time the field-meetings were plenty through the *Weſt* and through the *South*, and in the *North* and *Eaſt*. I began to have a great deſire to hear them ; for these Indulged, or these that had a *Tolleration* from the *Biſhop* and a *Presentation* from the *Patron* (as it was said that *Mr. Patterson* and *Mr. Sinclair* of *Ormiston* had), I say, though they were good men, and the people that heard them were edifyed by them, yet they were not so much countenanced of the Lord, and the ordinances dispensed by them had not that life and power that was in the persecuted meetings in the fields. For that *Indulgence* may be seen in the book entituled the *Hiſtory of the Indulgence*. I say, that when I had heard of these blefsed field-meetings, and having occasion to be *East* at *Dunse*, I got the opportunity of a field-meeting where *Mr. Henry Asbin* preached. His text was in *Deut.* xxxii. 15 :—*But* JESHURUN *waxed fat and kicked, and forsook the Lord, and lightly efteemed the Rock of his salvation;* which had so much effect on me that I longed to hear these men again; and when hearing *Mr. Patterson,* I found not that life in his preaching (though I had no prejudice at him nor any other, but only because they went on in finfull courses) I had found in that field-meeting.

14th Rem.—The meetings breaking up in the *South* beyond the *Stow* in *Gala-water,* I and another comerad went there; and *Mr. Thomas Wilkie,* who was afterward Minifter in the *Canon-gate Kirk,* entered here by *York's Tolleration.* But the thing to be remarked is, how the Lord was with the Minifters while they were with Him; for that day aforesaid he preached at a place called *Whitlie-burn-foot,* where there was so much of the Lord seen and felt that many spake of it afterward. And it was the Sabbath which *East Nisbet* communion was on. And the next Sabbath after, *Mr. John Welch* and *Mr. Richard Cameron* preached together at a place called the *Blew Cairn,* where *Mr. John Welch* baptized a man of twenty-eight years old. And it was very edifying and affecting to hear the man give his confeffion; and how the Minister caused him give confeffion of his faith, and caused him hold up his hand and swear to the *Solemn League* and *Covenant* and the *National Covenant.* O how sweet was that day when the Lord was amongft His people; and many a sweet day was then through the land, so that the land for some years might have been called *Jehovah-shammah: the Lord was there;* and the mountains, and hills, and burn-fides covered over with *Jehovah-jireh.* O what love and union was there. Likewise in this year, 1678, the *Highland Host* came to the *West* and preft a finfull bond; also the *Lowdon* Militia, which spoiled, robbed, and rifled many houses in the *West*, while the honeſt people there were living peaceably, only they were following the precious Gospel ordinances. But O what sympathy I had then with those who were persecuted (if ever I had any). So the Lord helped me to follow these persecuted field-meetings, and I found the Lord ; so that word was made out to me in *Isaiah* xl. 31 :—*They ſhall run and not be weary, they ſhall walk and not be faint.* O how sweetly would the people be telling their notes of the sermons which they had heard ; and how it was bleſt to their memory, and how their souls fed on the word which they heard. And when hearing these Miniſters, they were made to say, *Never man spake like this man.* At other times, people having such a deſire to feed upon the Lord's Word dispensed by these Miniſters, deſired not to speak to any till their soul had gotten the sap of the Word. One of these Miniſters, *Mr. Robert Gillespie,* having this note in his sermon,—*People will be in that frame that they deſire not to speak to any for a while,*—I found it so that day to my experience. O how did the Lord ſhine in these despised and persecuted field-meetings.

15*th Rem.*—I, with others, through the Lord's aſſiſtance, did follow these ordinances in that country-side without any debeatings, but being wholly taken up to hear and to be usefull to others. It pleased the Lord to ſtir up some in this country in *Mid-Lowdon,* and these my comerads, who were so eminent that I never thought myself comparable to them. For I thought aye myself the unworthieſt of these the Lord raised up to be inſtrumentall for bringing these persecuted preachings to *Lowdon.* So one dear comerad of mine (who, though he afterward differed in judgment, yet was dear to me ; for I allways thought him a choice Chriſtian), having a house and family, brought one of these persecuted Miniſters to his house ; and being too much lifted up with it, we did not give the Lord the glory as we ſhould have done. However, the Lord, who is gracious to pardon, did make that day's work the beginning of a good work in that country-side. For there were some on the *East* and *West* hand did joyn together, and had societys for that effect, and fetched south a Minifter to preach in the fields, and accordingly he did preach at *Cakemoor House*; it being the firft publick meeting we had (it was on the firft Sabbath of *January*, 1679), although there had been meetings in some houses. One meeting in *Pentland Hills* before this was broken, and the Minifter taken and some other prisoners. Yet I say, these meetings that broke up in that country, sometimes in *Crighton* Parifh, and sometimes in *Temple* Parifh and other Parifhes, the Lord did so wonderfully countenance and preserve them that, for the space of twenty-two or twenty-three Sabbath dayes and two week dayes, the enemies were so bounded that there was never any taken at these meetings, although we had them publickly on the hills called *Lowdon Edge*, or *Morphet Hills*. O how wonderfull was it to see and feel the joy of the Lord who was our ftrength. There was so much of the Lord seen at these meetings that very few who came to them did ever with good will return again to the dead and lifelefs Curates, till they were compelled, and some never went. It was also observed that many who came to these meetings (they were so blefsed of the Lord) were convinced and some converted, so that I hope the Lord, by the miniftry of these faithfull Minifters, brought in many to Himself; and others were civilized. And for the Parifh I was then in there were few who stayed with the Curate, which was good news to me; for I allways pityed them who heard these hirelings.

There was one thing remarkable, and it is this :—The Sabbath before *Lowdon Hill*, 1, with some others, went in to *Edinburgh* to seek a Minifter, but could by no means get one; and if we had had any meeting that day we could have scarcely escaped; for *Claverhouse* with a great deal of dragoons came all the way from *Lanrek* to *Lintoun*, through that range of *Morphet Hills*, so that there could have been no escaping : but the Lord outſhot the enemies in their own bow, and brake their deſigns. At these meetings, people were made to hear as they would have swallowed up the Miniſter, and Miniſters made to preach beyond their own expeɛtation ; and even some who were thought to be no great preachers, yet when they came forth with their lives in their hands, were wonderfully helped, so that they were scarcely thought to be these men ; so wonderfully did the Lord work with them and for them untill that breach fell in amongſt them concerning that wofull Church-rending and Church-waſting *Indulgence* (and they were about to silence *Mr. Richard Cameron* for preaching againſt it), likewise that diviſion which fell out at the communion at *Carrick* and at *Bothwell*, of which I shall give you some account.

16*th Rem.*—*Lowdon Hill*, as it was called, being fought the second Sabbath of June, and there being allways a resolution to gather up, so, after the defeat that was given there to *Claverhouse*, the word came through the country; and the honeſt people resolving to rise, I resolved to go and joyn with them. And hearing tell that some were for taking of horse from Curates and others, I had no freedom to take any man's horse, and went and agreed for a horse, which the man condescended to take again if I returned. So I went from that man's house to a place called *Malsly* in *Temple* Parish. And about the 3*rd or* 4*th of June* 1679, when we were gathering up, when we were taking our breakfast, my comerad's piſtol did go off, and shot me through the legg, where the ball did ſtick till it was cutt out. This was an ill presage. So I returned, and ſtayed sometimes in my brother's house, and sometimes in my mother's house, to and fro, my legg being twenty weeks in healing. But the thing I must take notice of is—when I was going there, viz., to *Bothwell*, I wondred to see men going so unconcerned ; for truly it was weighty to me when I conſidered such a weighty busineſs we were about. And then

E

when I thought I was to lose my life, it was not easy to me. And at that time I was in a very dead and lifelefs frame; and the Lord was hiding His face from me. And I was going from place to place; and the Sabbath on which *Bothwell Bridge* was fought, I was lying in a wood my alone, and heard the fhots from the *Caftle* for the victory, which the enemy had got, but was not so affected as I fhould have been. For I judged they might be broken, which was juftice on God's part for their not acknowledging the Church's defection, and for taking in the *Malignant* and *King's* interest when he had broken his *Oath* and *Covenant* both to God and man; for the people were loosed from their obligation to that *King* who had broken *Covenant;* and it was their fin in owning him after he had done so.

17*th Rem.*—My going from one place to another for fear of the enemy, and the hot weather, caused my legg to consume; for the matter fell down and did consume the flesh, till there was little but bones and sinews. But O, what of God might I have seen in such a wonderful outgate, for severals concluded that I would be a cripple. But such was the Lord's care and kyndnefs to me that with laying to of milk pottage where the tents were (there being five or six tents in my legg), it was cured. But even then, when my comerads were returned home, we stayed in houses where we were too much made of, and under all this stroak we grew very light and unconcerned with the Lord's work, then getting such a dash. However, the Lord, glory to His name, did not leave me in that sad condition, but did let me see my folly.

18*th Rem.*—One *Skeen*, being *Sheriff-depute*, sent to apprehend me, though I had not been at *Bothwell*, but becaufe I was going to it. And I had been several nights before in my mother's house; but that night they came I was, by the good providence of God, not in my mother's house, and so I escaped; but they abufed the house, and seized upon anything I had.

In this year, 1679, on the 14*th of Auguft, Mr. John Kid* and

Mr. John King were execute, and on that same day they dyed, there was an *Indemnity*, and a *Proclamation.* The *Proclamation* was this which you may see in that book intituled, THE BANDERS DISBANDED:—*We bind and oblige us conjunctly and severally, our Heirs and Succefsors, that the said shall live peaceably, and in order thereto we bind and oblige us to present him before his Majesty's Privy Councill when we shall be called so to do; and in case of failty in not presenting him, we shall be lyable to pay the sum of* 6000 *merks.* This was something of the bond that the cautioners were to give. This was practised in *Newbottle,* where *Mr. George Johnston* did accept of that dreadfull *Indemnity;* and many of the Parifh of *Newbottle* were cautioners. One of them said *Mr. Johnston* was over free : another that difsented said, *Why should he not be free?* He answered again, *Do you not know that we are cautioners?* O, a dreadfull ftep of the church's defection, which the Lord helped me and several others to witnefs againft ; for though I heard him in the fields, yet when he was limited, I did not hear him, but teftified againft it. So after the Lord recovered my legg, which had been very sore, I went to the meetings that were in the houses ; for the minifters would not preach but in or near houses, after the defeat at *Bothwell.* It would have broken a tender heart to see those who had been so free and faithfull to difplay a banner, either in house or field, so suddenly changed ; for it was very observable that the prefence of the Lord departed; neither Minifters nor people were in that frame as before. However, I, with some others, went to them ; but found a great alteration, both as to freedom and faithfullnefs. And we were always speaking to them, and found them all yielding to that *Indemnity* (though they did not so cordially embrace it as some did that got the bond, as *Mr. Johnston,* and others), excepting *Mr. Richard Cameron,* *Mr. Donald Cargil,* and *Mr. Thomas Douglas,* yet he left the other two and went away after the firft *Sanquhar Declaration.*

19*th Rem.*—After I recovered, and began to work, the enemy

came again seeking me; and I, finding no safety, wandred from one place to another.   At laſt I began to think of merchandizing, so that I might go from place to place, because I found myself not safe in my mother's house.   Yet I defigned not God's glory as I ſhould have done, but my own gain.   So I beſtowed all my money at *Lanrek*, which was the beginning of my merchandizing; and, leaving no money to pay my expence upon the way going to *Moffat*, I was very destitute, and was afraid, because the troopers were lying in that country, and having no money and night drawing on, and few houses on the way.   But I met with a young man who, after some discourse, brought me home to his father's house, where I got some acquaintance, which I looked upon as the Lord's providence when I was deſtitute among hills.

About this year, viz.— 1679, debeats fell in amongſt us about *Indulgences*, and the *Indemnity* after *Bothwell*, and did still increase among profeſsors and miniſters ; however, I bleſs the Lord for it, he helped me to own the honeſt side, and preserved me from the right hand extreams which I saw to be wrong in that sorcerer, *Gib*, who, with some others, went to the hills.   One of them, *Isobel Calender*, went with him, and would not stay to keep her own child, though very young (I suppose sucking), and left her father, though a good man, her husband being execute.   It was a great mercy and a wonder that there were not many carried away with them, viz.—*Gib's* folk, as they were called : firſt, because they seemed to be the most zealous and weighted of any then in the land.   One of them, named *Ann Stewart*, said to my wife, they muſt take 24 hours for prayer, and yet afterwards would blaspheme terribly ; secondly, confidering the grounds miniſters gave the people to stumble in their being greatly changed, both as to freedom and faithfullneſs in preaching.   For when we had gone to *Edinburgh*, to deſire them to come forth and preach, they did enquire if they would get a house to preach in or at, and would not go to the fields as formerly ; but people being so throng upon other in houses, some would have been to be carryed out. All this and more than I write was very ſtumbling. One instance I give : *Mr. John Anderson*, sometime miniſter in the *Weſt Kirk*, one time through persuaſion went freely from a house and ſtood leaning upon his ſtaff and preached ; but he was severely censured, and said (as I heard), we would not get him to the fields again.

20th Rem.—After *Mr. Douglas* came from *Mr. Cameron*, I rode south with him and heard *Mr. Hepburn* preach ; and that Sabbath there was a meeting at *Mount Lowdon* ; but there came a company of dragoons and scattered the meeting. And there were several taken, but they did get away again ; and the miniſter escaped by hiding himself among the corn. And so I, being absent that day, escaped ; and all the preachings we had were never scailled with troopers except that day. And for all this while (as I said), I was ſtill hearing the ministers, but with a sore heart.

21st Rem.—In the year 1681, it pleased the Lord again to lay His hand upon me. When I was in my mother's house I had a great pain in my head, and a sore throat ; and I did sweat in the mornings till my shirt was as if it had been in the water. Yet I was forced to rise, otherwise it was like to be my death ; and although the dragoons had been seeking me before, yet the Lord preserved me all the while I was not well, which was a considerable time. And when it pleaſed the Lord to recover me again, I went about my employment of merchandizing, though with many difficulties.

In this year, 1681, *July 27th, Mr. Donald Cargil* was execute. I had allways a respeƈt for the honeſt cauſe and for that difsenting party, though I did not joyn with them with them till afterward ; but was hearing the miniſters, though with much difsatisfaction. One time when I was deſiring a minister to come out and preach in the country, he said, that *Mr. Donald Cargil* was the worst fight that ever the *Church* of *Scotland* saw ; with what satisfaƈtion could I hear then? In the year 1681, on the *8th day of Auguſt,* I subscribed with my hand to be the Lord's.

22nd Rem.—Then, in the next year, viz., 1682, while following my employment, I had great debeats with the miniſters; for they did allways condemn that poor party for the *Declaration* at *Lanrck,* which was this year *Jany.* 12*th.* One of them, viz., *Mr. Barcly,* said the like of that doth no good. I went sometimes to hear them, yet with great reluctance, and sometimes not. I was going one time to hear, and by the way the miniſter, *Mr. Alexander Burnet,* said to me, that *Mr. Richard Cameron* was no more a Presbyterian than the horse he rode upon. At this time the persecution and tryall was great. I do not remember any more remarkable things this year.

23rd Rem.—In the year 1683, *Mr. Donald Cargil* being dead, we had then no publick preachings; for those miniſters that were for preaching in houses, laid by, and keeped up no publick *Teſtimony,* and some turned merchants. Only *Mr. John Rae* used sometimes to come to *Temple* Pariſh, and sometimes *Mr. John Hepburn.* I heard them when I heard none of the rest that were condemning the *Testimony* that was keeped up by theſe *Declarations.* And the laſt of theſe I heard, for ought I know, was *Mr. Hepburn,* at *Malſlie,* when he reckoned those that had caſten off the Magiſtrates and Miniſters, amongſt proud doers, though at this time these called Magiſtrates were turned tyrants. About this time I began to joyn with the Societys that had withdrawn from the generality of the Ministers, upon the account of their complyance with the enemy in not going forth to preach faithfully and freely as they had done formerly. For I had continued with them for some more than three years, hearing them with little satisfaction; for, as I said, I had sad debeats with them; and this I write that it may be known we did not withdraw from hearing without ground; for many a sore heart I and others had with them. So I did withdraw from hearing for a little time, and joyned in

Societys about *Pentland*, and the *Temple* Parifh, having great debeats with my old and dear comerads, especially one who was very dear to me ; for though he was strict againfl the *Indulgences* (year 1669), and the *Indemnity* (year 1679), yet that unhappy difference fell in among us about withdrawing and not withdrawing from the Miniflers, as they were then flated, for there were' none of them keeping up a publick *Testimony*, by preaching in any place where they were called, but they lurked and laid by.

About this time there were some articles drawn up for regulating the Societys, and some queflions to be afked at them who were to be brought into the Societys. This rule had not been amongfl us for many years before, if at all fince the *Reformation*. So, when at a meeting these queflions were read, the forementioned comerad flumbled and said they imposed upon us and excluded us from hearing Ministers, while they were only to keep out the scandalous and ignorant, and that we might not have such loose persons in Society as formerly we had, when every person was admitted, if they could pray. It was a grief to see persons admitted to open their mouth to the Lord who could scarce speak sense, and spoke unbecomingly of God in prayer; for prayer is only speaking to God, and not of God. I do not say but I have been guilty of this myself; but I would defire to guarde againfl it, as a thing very improper. About this time, *Mr. James Renwick* came home out of *Holland*, an ordained Minister (it seemed strange that the great and godly men that were in this Church would not ordain him, except he would be limited and bounded) ; and he continued in the work of his Ministry untill he was taken and execute, *Feb.* 17*th*, 1688.

24*th Rem.*—In the year 1684, after *Mr. James Renwick* had been preaching, what through misformation, and one thing and another, I did separate for a time, and joyned with the party that was for *Mr. John Flint;* for I thought they were a tender party, and so they were, for they had much of the gift of prayer, and of the spirit of prayer. They were also for changing the names of the dayes of the week and months of the year; but this thing being not reformed when the Church was in her power and purity, I thought it not sufficient ground of separation. This party said that *Mr. Renwick* was perjured, upon the account of his telling some things that they thought should not have been told till these persons had been under that same secresy; for there was something of an oath of secresy at that time, because the wrestling remnant could get nothing done when they had any *Declaration* or *Teſtimony* to emitt, but the enemys got notice of it. So, as I said, through that and other things, I did withdraw for a time, which was not right in me; though I am not convinced, if the Church were in power, but the foresaid dayes and months should be changed, yet should not separate upon such grounds. All the time I was with that party of *James Ruſsell* and *Mr. Flint*, I seemed to be tender; for *Mr. Flint* came home out of *Holland*, not an ordained minister; he had only a testimonial of his learning. So I and others heard him, which was not right in us, and to have weakened the hands of the other party that were carrying on the *Teſtimony* with *Mr. Renwick*; for they were the only suffering remnant. And yet how ready was I and others to be carryed away at the right hand; so, except the Lord preſerve us, we are ready to go off at the right hand as well as at the left hand : sometimes running from one snare we fall into another snare. So I continued, sometimes debeating both with the remnant who were suffering with *Mr. Renwick*, and with the profeſsors. In this year, and for two years after, there was little or no publick preaching; for the perſecution was very hot, and many were forced to flee, some into *England*, and some into *Holland*. At this time there were *Circuit Courts* throughout the most part of the *South* and *Weſt* of *Scotland*.

25*th Rem.*—At this time, when all my comerads were forced to flee, yet the Lord preserved me from the hands of the enemy (and I still followed my employment, though with no great prosperity), which I looked upon as a wonder ; and I have cause to magnify the Lord upon the remembrance of it. When others either complyed and went to the Curates, or were forced to flee, I was only obliged to come to my mother's house when it was late, and to go early away again, and so I was preserved, for which I blefs the Lord.

26th Rem.—My great fear at this time was left I fhould be taken, and that I had not wherewith to pay my debt ; but the Lord, who many a time disappointed me of my fears, disappointed me of this also. For one ·night when I was lying on my bed in a barn in *Pentland*, where I now dwell, that word came to me in a dream,—*Believe in the Lord, so fhall ye prosper;* and after that I thought things went some better with me, though I was low enough in the world. In this year, 1684, the *Apologeticall Declaration* was fixed upon *Market Crofses* and *Kirk* doors. Then the persecution arose very hot ; yet, while I wandered from one place to another, the Lord preserved me, which was wonderfull. And sometimes, when I had any little businefs more than ordinary, as in the time of selling lint seed, I found and saw the malice of the enemys reftrained, so that I was not much troubled with them ; and this was observed by onlookers; for some would have said in jeft, when they had seen me publickly about my mother's house, *It seems it is lint-seed time, or tar time.* And I observed that the Lord reftrained the enemys, for it was much to win through and to get myself maintained. Though friends were kind to me, yet my relations were oftentimes afraid that I fhould be seen about the house.

27th Rem.—In the year 1685 the persecution grew hotter and hotter ; for at this time the *Oath* of *Abjuration* was prefsed upon all in some places, both men and women ; and it came to that that there was none that durft travell upon the highwayes except they had a pafs. And then it was a time of perplexity : as in that Scripture, *Isaiah* xxviii. 8 :—*All tables are full of vomit, and*

F

there is no place clean; so that there was scarcely a family that I might go into and ftay all night where they had not taken the *Oath.* And how perplexing it was then how to carry and how to go to these houses and familys that had taken the *Oath*, for I scrupled to ftay all night and joyn with them in their exercise. However, the Lord, who provided for me formerly, provided for me then, there being two or three houses, where I did moft refide in, that were free of that *Oath.* I might keep no publick market to buy and sell in, as in the *Rev.* xiii. 16, 17 :—*None might buy and sell but those that had the mark of the beaft.* I did sometimes resort to *Pentland*, where fhe who is now my wife did dwell. There was some difference then in our judgment about *Mr. James Renwick* and *Mr. Flint.* She was very usefull in these times both to me and many others ; for be of what judgment they will, if fhe thought they were godly, fhe intertained them. Yet fhe had allways (from the time the Lord dealt with her) the greateft love to them that were moft honeft for the LORD JESUS. For there were at that time three or four parties, yet none were suffering honeftly but those that were adhering to the *Teftimonys* of *Sanquhar* and *Lanrek;* for they suffered for their adhering to that GREAT TRUTH THAT JESUS CHRIST IS THE ONLY HEAD AND KING of His own Church and people, and for their adhering to the *Covenants*, which their *Teftimony* doth witnefs, also for disowning the *King's* authority. In this year there were about thirty men that had the lap of their ears cut off, and they with others were banifhed to *Jamaica.* In this year also was the *Declaration* againft the proclaiming of the *Duke* of *York*, 28*th* of *May.* And I was not clear at this time to joyn with them that came over with *Argyle*, for reasons which are in the *Vindication*, which I defire to adhere to. In this year I renewed my *Covenant* with the Lord, wherein I dedicated the tenth of all that the Lord had given me to His people, His use and service.

28*th Rem.*—In the year 1686, after I had withdrawn some time from *Mr. Renwick* (as I said before) upon the account of the wrong information I had from *Mr. Flint*, yet I found that they were the only party that were witneffing against both right and left hand extreams, and gave *Teftimony* against *Mr. Flint* for the way of his entry into the work of the Miniftry, for his marrying and offering to baptize (which I and my comerad, with some in *Fife* did oppose), when he had only a teftimonial of his learning from abroad. So, when I knew this, I went again to *Mr. Renwick*, and heard him when he was preaching at *Brades Craigs;* and I continued hearing him till he died. One time, when I was hearing him not long after this, I narrowly escaped ; as I have done many a time, so at this time particularly. I had come into a house, and I was scarce well gone out, when the *Bailife* of *Nicolson*, one who was at *Bothwell Bridge* (his name was *George Cunninghame*) came in, having *Sir William Nicolson's* orders to apprehend me, saying—*Where is that rascall ?* and many other such railling words. And *Sir William* was very violent, for the Curate, called *Burgefs*, set him on against me ; and he, with his brother, *Sir John*, often threatened to put me out of the town, there being few or none in the town but what had complyed and gone to the Curate ; yet it was so ordered of the Lord that I was in it when they were both dead ; and it came so to pafs that neither of them nor theirs had a furr of land in that town. It is to be remarked, as the judgment of God upon this *Sir William Nicolson*, for his persecution and other wickednefses, he being a very great swearer and a blasphemer, that his senses were taken from him. . . . And the said *Bailife* some years after was forced to flee from his own house naked for debt.

At this time, in the end of the year 1686, there were some Minifters came forth who had been lurking and lying by, and were condemning those that were carrying on the *Teftimony* with *Mr. Renwick* and afterward *Mr. Alexander Shields*, and preached, some in houses and some in the fields in the night time, yet were not enhancing the *Teftimony*, as it was stated by the honeft party; but when they saw the *Duke* of *York* was likely to give them any liberty, they were beginning to pray for him as their lawfull *King*, which they did openly the year following. Yet all this time the Lord preserved me from joyning with these Minifters, though I was wo when I saw some people going away quietly in the night-time. And the Lord helped the honeft party in the land to wit-nefs against them, by *Mr. Renwick* preaching publickly either in the night or in the day. All this while we keeped up private meetings.

About this time I had a very sore pain in my throat, and I thought it would be my death ; but the Lord that delivered me out of many troubles, delivered me out of this also, for it brake and I was eased. There were few years fince the Lord took a dealing with me, but He was aye hedging in my wayes, either with pains or sicknefs ; but O the Lord was aye both good and kind, although I had provoked Him both publickly and privately. And I confefs I was a great undervaluer of precious CHRIST, and did intertain my lufts and idols in the Lord's room, and did not walk worthy of the Lord, as I ought to have done.

29th Rem.—About this time I had a defire to be married, for I saw it a thing warrantable and commendable ; and the Lord guided me in it; for though I was sometimes thinking of others, yet, when I came seriously to think of it, I thought I could marry none but the woman I got, viz., *Helen Alexander*, to whom I was married, *Nov.* 30*th*, 1687, by *Mr. James Renwick;* and I have cause to blefs the Lord that so wonderfully provided such a match for me.

30th Rem.—In this year, 1687, the *Duke* of *York* sent out some *Proclamations* of *Liberty* and *Tolleration*, which was a dreadfull step of the Church's defection. There were many Minifters that had escaped the former snares of the *Indulgence* and *Indemnity* after *Bothwell*, yet were taken in this fearfull snare ; and yet some

of the Minifters said to myself that this year was the beginning of
the Church's delivery, and I wondred when they said it. But I
wifh that they may have seen the ill of it; but their own things
blinded them, for it was a time when they got their settled
ftipends. And so far was it from the beginning of a delivery to
the work and cause of God that to me and many others, whose
eyes the Lord had opened, it seemed the beginning of a greater
bondage and barring of the Lord's work. But what is said in the
Hind let Loose, in the *Protestation against the publick Resolutions,*
and by *Mr. James Renwick* in his *Teftimony,* is much more than
what I can say, to all which I adhere and refer. So I say it was
a great step of our Church's defection; though the beginning of
all these fearfull fteps was in the year 1650, which you will see in
Protestation against the publick Resolutions for bringing in the
Malignants to places and power, and preliminting afsemblies both
as to matter and members. But I cannot write what contendings
I and others had about that *Tolleration.* There were many profefsors who took a deteftation at it, though the Minifters con-
tended strongly for it, because it was for their own worldly
intereft, as in that place in *Isaiah—Will ye plant me amongst my
people for handfulls of barley and pieces of bread?* The forecited
books being so full to hold the iniquity of this *Tolleration,* I have
little to write; but their new holding was of men and not of the
Lord Jesus. For, to my uptaking, those who entered to their
congregations by virtue of that absolute power that the *Tolleration* came from, were not entering in by Jesus Chrift, which is the
door, but were climbing up some other way, and so may be
called thieves and robbers; for, when these preachers came to
preach, one must run or ride and acquaint the next Magiftrate,
though at that time the most part of them were wicked malignant
men, who cared little either for them or their preaching; they
were to tell the Minifter's name, so he must not preach anything
that might alienate the hearts of the hearers from the *King* (that

Popifh Tyrant) or his *Government*. But, O what wreftling then had the poor remnant which the law was left in full force against, and wo I and others had to see and hear how this wicked *Tolleration* was applauded and defended. One time I heard *Mr. David Walker* (who afterwards was Minifter in *Temple* Parifh, and did enter into that congregation by virtue of that *Tolleration*) praying for that *Popifh Tyrant;* though I never heard him preach in that congregation, for I verbally (as the Lord helped me to be an instrument to bring the persecuted Minifters and persecuted Gospel to that Parifh, and it had been blefsed of the Lord to them, yea, some of them were brought in to Jesus Chrift) did protest against his entering to that congregation by virtue of that *Tolleration*, which exonered me in some measure. But for ought I know his ministry was not succefsfull ; for though they said that that time was their delivery, yet I can affirm it that the persecuted field-meetings were so blefsed of the Lord that it had more effect in that Parifh and the Parishes about in one year than it had for seventeen years after. For the people grew rather worse under their ministry ; so it may be said it was a time of their getting good benefices and ease, but not a time of the Lord's bringing in sinners to Himself—but more of this afterward. But as the Lord had guided me formerly, so now He guided me wonderfully ; for the persecution was very hot against both Ministers and profefsors who did not comply with that wofull *Tolleration*, which the Lord preserved me from ; though as to personall sins I was guilty as to too much worldliness, and much given to fall asleep in the time when others were praying ; for we had our fellowship meetings in the night-time, for fear of the enemys, after the example of our Lord's disciples. Yet I would defire it of all Christians (because of our weakness, and being apt to deadness and fleep especially in the night) rather to have their meetings for prayer and conference in the day-time (if there be no fear of enemys), whatever hindrance it may prove to our worldly bufinefs. So, about this time, I was married, which if I had improven to God's glory, I may say my lot fell in a pleasant place; but, what through fear of wanting in my married life, I was very bent upon the world, and too anxious. And many times I did break out in passion, to the dishonour of God and of religion, *Satan* working with my corruption, which was my sin in yielding to the temptations so much as I did. Which I defire all to guard against, as they would not be found grievers of the Lord, as alas I was, and bring upon themselves and their posterity many rods and crofses. Though I defire to believe that it was that which He threatened when I closed with Him, as it is in *Psalm* lxxxix. 33 :— *Yet will I not take my loving-kindnefs from him;* yet I would defire all that profefs religion to beware of sin because His grace abounds. So I went on, as the Lord enabled me, to witnefs against that *Tolleration;* and likewise my wife and children.

31*st Rem.*—Some short time after I was married, the *Vindication* was printed, and some of them came to our house to be sold. And at this time the Papists were advanced to publick places. And among the rest, *James Clark, Laird* of *Wright-houses,* who came to our house seeking for uncustomed goods, found about twelve of the foresaid books, and carried them straight to the *Abbey* to the *Chancellour,* who was the *Earl* of *Perth,* a Papist. Also about this time *Mr. Renwick* was taken; and some of them were brought to him in the prison, and he owned them. However, it put me and my wife in some fear; and it was wonderfull, confidering the wickednefs of that time, that they did not send out to apprehend us. But the Lord, who many times delivered me, restrained them, so that we were not troubled; yet, for our own safety, we lay not in our own house.

In this year, 1688, on the 17*th* of *February, Mr. Renwick* was execute. The drums did beat all the time after he set his foot upon the scaffold till he was caft over. However, he was carried through honourably, and was faithfull to the death, to the conviction of many that branded him as a Jesuit. And many Minifters and profefsors said he died in an error ; and these Minifters went on in their wicked courfes, although he had given a *Testimony* againft that wofull *Tolleration*, and sealed it with his blood. *Mr. John Flint*, leaving his former ftrictnefs, joyned with the reft, and was ordained, *January*, 1689 (but neither he nor any of the Minifters preached againft the taking away of *Mr. Renwick's* life). I had sometimes a debeat with him, and told him that he was not following Presbyterian principles.

About this time I took a great cold, which caft me in ficknefs, but the Lord recovered me again. In *October*, 1688, I was seized again with great pains through my body, with a great fhortnefs of breath, and I was very near to death ; but the Lord had mercy on me ; for, with His blefsing, upon the drawing of blood, I recovered again ; but I had ftill some fhortnefs of breath.

About this time, on *November 29th*, 1688, my oldeft son *James*, was born, while I was ftill unwell, which was a sore tryall to my dear wife. And in my ficknefs and pain I took an efking, which severalls concluded would be my death ; but as I said, the Lord brought me through. And when my child was baptized (for Providence ordered it so that *Mr. Thomas Linning*, whom we had then a freedom to hear, came to our house to ftay all night, about the 11*th of December* 1688, and baptized him, preaching on the 15th of *John*), I was so weak that I could not hold him up. And on this same night some men went over to *Roflyn Caftle*, and burnt their images, and many of their Popifh books, I telling them where they would find their *Priests' Robes* ; but withall, I defired some to go over after them and hinder them from taking or hurting anything except what belonged to their *Idolatry*: for at this time the *Prince of Orange* was come to *England*.

At this time, *Mr. Alexander Shields* and *Mr. David Houston* went through the country, and preached (where they got a call) faithfully againſt that anti-chriſtian *Tolleration*, and againſt all ſin-full confederacies, inſiſting very much in their doctrine againſt ſin-full aſſociations, condemning them from Scripture. And the Lord was with them, while they abode with Him ; for I suppose there were scarce any who preached so eminently againſt ſin as *Mr. Shields* did. And yet afterwards he fell into that same ſin he had preached so much againſt ; for the main scope of his doctrine did run againſt the joyning with the time abominations, as the said *Tolleration* and *Indulgences;* and so did *Mr. David Houſton;* and they were much for encouraging the honeſt handfull to ſtand at a diſtance from these evills, and from the *Eraſtian Indulgence* which ministers had accepted of. One time I heard *Mr. David Houston*, preaching in the *Merse*, say, that we ſhould soon be quite of *Popery* and *Prelacy*, but not of *Supremacy* and *Eraſtianism*. For at that time *Popery* and *Prelacy* were at a great height. About two years after, the Lord brought down *Prelacy*; and in this year *Popery* was brought down; and the *Duke* of *York* was forced to flee, the Lord deserting him and his great army. And he, for-saking the *Government*, fled into *France*, as a just judgment on him for his aſſuming to himself an absolute power, which is blasphemy in any creature. But *Supremacy* laſted longer, and the honeſt party had it to wreſtle with many years, as will be seen afterward when the Lord diſcovers the iniquity of these times. About this time, *Mr. Shields*, *Mr. Linning*, and *Mr. Boyd* joyned together. *Mr. Houſton* went to *Ireland*, and left the united Societies here in *Scotland*, they judging that he failed when he promised and did not keep his word. Yet, when he was in *Ireland*, he witneſſed against the sins of the time, and I expect he dyed well. So the foresaid three continued preaching; but *Mr. Boyd* was not so straight in the Lord's cause as he ſhould have been, for *Mr. Renwick* was jealous of him, and his fear came to paſs ; for he was a great inſtrument of taking the other two off their former ground, and proved but a naughty man. For he caused to proclaim the

G

Prince of Orange's Declaration, which was the first step of that
honeſt party's being taken off their feet, which that, and what they
did afterward will manifest; for then they began to have meetings
with the Ministers that had been under *York's Tolleration,* and had
been lurking and lying by from a publick *Testimony.*

Letters from Sir Robert Hamilton* to Helen Alexander & James Currie.

———◦∙✪∙◦———

LETTER I.

To *Helen Alexander*, Spouse to *James Currie*, Merchant in *Pentland*, upon the death of her dear Son, *Thomas Currie*.

Dear Chriſtian Friend,—Tho' both time and weaknefs ſtraitens me, yet I could not omit this occaſion. Your trial (I ſhall not say my own, that not once is to be compared with yours), hath been ſharp ſince our laſt meeting ; but well are we that our crofs is both of Chriſt's çhoofing, ordering and managing : and O, ſtrange to fleſh and blood, that the more heavy, the more bitter and ſharp it be, the more proper for us.   It lets us find where our leprous botch and boil lies ; for were our back whole, our burden would be the more light and easy: but it is our boil there that makes it uneasy, and us kick and fling under it; yea, further, the more we are made to see and dwell under the mismanagements of

---

* SIR ROBERT HAMILTON was a zealous Covenanter.   He commanded the Covenanting forces at Drumclog and Bothwell Bridge, and afterwards took ✿ prominent part in the organization of the Societies of the persecuted people. A procefs of forfeiture was pafsed againſt him by the Privy Council in 1683, and he was sentenced to be executed without trial in the event of his apprehenſion ; but he lived till 1701.   After the Revolution he was imprisoned by the Government on account of his ſtrict Cameronian principles.   He died at Borrowſtounefs, Oct. 21, 1701, at the age of 51.

our crofs, we may conclude that the more dexterously it is composed for us; for thereby we are led to see what miserable comforters we are in the time of need, either to ourselves or these most dear to us, and what need there is of momentaneous influences from the great Physician, not only to bear our crofs, but to guide ourselves and others under it. And this is one of His main defigns in afflicting His, to keep them empty about His hand, and to employ Him in all, both as to the matter and manner of our affairs or afflictions, to take with our finfulnefs, senselefsnefs, and stupidity, in both helping and extricating ourselves or others; that He may get the sole trust, credit, and employment, both as to the care, management, or accomplifhing of His own unspotted and tender defigns towards us. This was His way with *Martha* and *Mary*, whom He loved, yet tarried after their fending to Him. Why, O what a difcovery thereby made He of their folly, misjudgings of themselves, yea, rather of His blefsed self, with the misjudgings of the other difciples. No doubt these poor women thought they were fhort in not sending oftener to Him; yea, it stays not here, but questioned both His power and tendernefs in not coming sooner, and that now He had fitten His time; and the other disciples, they'll die with *Lazarus*: even Chrift Himself they think, can be no comfort to them when *Lazarus* was gone. O, how loves Satan to fish in muddy water; to draw poor things from the very end and defign of Chrift in the crofs, to rob them both of the peaceable fruit and fweetnefs thereof.

But, dear friend, I truft that the Lord will fruftrate the enemy, and raise you up in due time, and make you find, see, and say that all His ways are good towards you, and that *all things*, even your own real mismanagements, *shall work together for your good*, wean you more from yourself, and all self-confidence, from all Time's things, comforts, and delights, and so a seeing, an infinite up-making, with an all-sufficiency of relief, peace, comfort, and consolation in Himself. But I muft defift. My head is yet very weak. I design to see you shortly. I am not able to write to your kind husband. I refer him to *Mr. Kid* and *Thomas Gillespie's* letters. My love to all your kind and sweet family. The Lord Himself be with you all. In hafte, *Your affured and affectionate friend and sympathiser,* R. HAMILTON.

Borrowstounnefs, April 29, 1698.

LETTER II.

To *Helen Alexander,* Spouse to *James Currie,* after the death of her dear Son, *James Currie.*

My dear sympathifing Christian Friend,—Tho' it is seldom I am able to write, and at beft with great pain, yet I am in a great measure constrained to this fhort line. You seem to me yet to drive heavily under various discouragements. What are you doing? Are you suffering the enemy to make a pack-horse of you? Are you fiding with that inveterate enemy againft your sweet Lord, His will and way with you and yours? O, do you think you could have managed better than He has done? Let not such thoughts once enter, but with horror and indignation. Can ye not say, *He has done all things well,*—ye will be made both to see and say it. Fall on another way of it, of prizing Him above all, and praifing Him for all, and you will find a fweet life of it; yea, it fhall prove a door of hope—a door of entrance for a pleafant life of it in your old days. You may safely credit Him; put a blank in His hand; He can, He will do you no wrong; *tho' He cause grief, yet He will have compaffion,* according to His tender mercies. Has He said that *all things,* even of crofses and afflictions, *fhall tend for the good of them that love* and fear *Him?* O, what a cordial is this! and what a noble commentary to expone the darkest and heaviest like dispensations we may be tryfted with; and hath this come forth from His sweet lips, and shall we not fit down and sing over it, and singly and cordially fay, *The cup which my Father hath given me, fhall I not drink it ?* It was our Lord's own words when about to grapple with His Father's wrath, and the all of the wrath of man ; yet to make your cup easy He took up His heartsomely, with a, *Shall I not drink it ?* yea, I will drink the bitter dregs of it that they may but taste of the brim of it. O, my dear friend, is not *His yoke easy and His burden light*, besides what it was to Him. O, prize and praise, employ credit and trust, and lay and leave yourself and all your cares, fears, and troubles on Him, and this is the way to please Him and eafe your soul. I can say no more. Himself be with you, and all your sweet family. I am, *your affured friend*,   R. HAMILTON.

March 17, 1701.

LETTER III.

To *James Currie*, Merchant in *Pentland*.

Chriftian Friend,—Having this occafion, I could not but salute you and your bed-fellow with a line. Our night seems to grow still darker and darker, and will do, I think, till the day break ; for I can see nothing but still more and more confirmations that nothing but judgments will decide *Zion's* controversy ; for see we not that fin and all manner of abominations has free scouth to range and rage at random without oppofition and contradiction, whereas precious truth no sooner begins to gaunt, rax, ftretch, or rouse itself in the grave, tho' never so faintly, but all ranks— kings, princes, priests, and people—are all armed, affrighted, pro- voked, and irritated, and new discoveries of hatred, malice, dis- satisfaction, and enmity appears in their tongues, countenances, and actions. But no wonder that the adulterer and adulteress, the thief and robber, are ever made to flee the light, which might both discover and be a mean to apprehend them. I find the great ones, with the clergy, speak with one tongue ; they find they are truth-bitten, and they know of no other mean but to lick themselves whole again with their own tongues, calling the late Declaration * nonsensical, and what not. But let them call it what they will, they were never so stung nor galled with anything, as some of their own accomplices have been made to drop from them ; but let them say and think of it what they will, great peace have I in what is done ; and I trust the Lord has set to His seal to it, as an acceptable sacrifice in His fight. Now, dear friends, when the Lord is coming to pull down what He hath built, and to pluck up what He hath planted, and to bring evil upon all flefh, O but it be much the duty of His poor people not to seek great things for themselves. We are not behind if we keep clean garments, tho' cloathed with the reproaches of Christ ; and if we can have a peaceable conscience, which will be a feaft unto us, tho' kept between hand and mouth otherways, and put to grapple with the frowns, down-lookings, malice, and hatred of open enemies and profefsed friends. They know little of the emptinefs of a deceitful world, and of the soul-satisfaction and consolation to be found in Christ who will not come from that *Lebanon* to enjoy His company. We are but strangers and pilgrims on earth ; and we need not think much if it be not kindly to us. O sweet, sweet word,—Verily, *there is a reft prepared for the people of God.*

My love and respects to yourself, bed-fellow, and family, and to all my dear Chriftian friends at *Edinburgh.* Hoping you will mind us, who defire to commend and commit you to the Lord, and remain *your afsured Friend,* ROB. HAMILTON.

Dec. 17, 1695.

* " The Declaration of a poor, wasted, misrepresented remnant of the suffering, anti-Popish, anti-Prelatick, anti-Erastian, anti-Sectarian, true Presbyterian Church of Chrift in Scotland, united together in a general correspondence," publifhed at Sanquhar, the 10th of August, 1692.

LETTER IV.

To *James Currie*, Merchant in *Pentland*.

Dear Chriſtian Friend,—To forget you were both unnatural and un-chriſtian. I confeſs you and your family have been encouraging and refreſhing, not only when present with you, but my reflection on it when at a diſtance. But alas! what can I write, what can I say ;—*The Lord's ways are in the deep waters, and His paths are paſt finding out;* and yet I doubt not both legible and inſtructing and ſtrengthening to some. But O such are rare ; few fearing Him, and few upon His secrets. Ah, how may this in a great measure be our lamentation,—*We have not a prophet among us, nor any that know how long.* Lord keep us from wearying. O to be waiting on Him. But ah, we may fear that on-waiters will be few ; yet bleſsed ſhall they be, tho' but one, that ſhall wait it out. They ſhall be made to see and say that *He has done all things well,* and all the pains and coſt of these times have been but small in comparison of that noble result and enriching income it shall yield and produce. But O wrath ! wrath at the door, againſt a perfidious, profane, hypocritical Christ's-cause-and-people-betraying generation. *Who ſhall be able to abide the day of His coming?* O for hearts to fear, hear, and draw near a holy and ſin-revenging God. Ah! His holineſs and juſtice are vilipended, His name is trampled upon, His works and ways flouted at and disdained ; the monuments of enemies ruint, and His people's deliverances forgotten and misimproven. O dear friend, when I win to think of my base ingratitude, it makes my heart to bleed within. O what has He done for some, and how badly requited.

Let me hear from you, and how it is with you all. My love to yourself and bed-fellow, and to all the sweet children ; and the

blefling of the Lord be with you all. I hope ye will mind us.—
I remain *your afsured Friend,*   ROBERT HAMILTON.
Bridge-nose, June 9th, 1697.

LETTER V.

To *James Currie,* Merchant in *Pentland.*

Chriftian and dear Friend,—I am ever glad to hear of you and
your family's welfare, so I would be very defirous to have a line
from you now and then.

Mr. Kid has been very diligent in performing your line anent
me. O to have this enemy, *Self,* more and more subdued, that
His will and way with me were more my delight. But O, silly
worm that I am, that would be content to be more denied to one
piece of self, to have another piece of it somewhat gratified—to
have my allowance diminished, providing I could have it anothei
way. But He will have His people know that that piece of the
crofs their stomachs stands most at, is the very thing that can
least be wanting : yea, without it, it would be no crofs; and, if
no crofs, what creatures would we be ; yea, what noble experi-
ences and promises should the poor thing be robbed of. Then,
dear friend, nothing to a full resignation and upgiving of ourselves to Him, to His tutory, guiding and disposal, and closely
following Him thro' thorns, seas, rocks, and mountains, and
wherever He goes. It is poor thoughts and esteem we have of
Him when His company is not prized beyond all hazards and
difficulties that can attend it ; and when not seen in His tutory,
leading, and disposing, as infinite in power, love, and wisdom.
O brother, let us set to to keep Him high ; for tho' we should
never see a better of it in time, to get leave to serve Him, tho' in
the meanest of His service, is a reward above what men or angels
can give ; yea, He and His despised cause will yet win the day.
H

O to wait without wearying, fainting, offending, or making haste. My respects to your kind bed-fellow and family. Now, mind us, and God's blefling be with you all.—I am, dear Friend, *yours sympathizing,*   R. HAMILTON.

Borrowſtounneſs, Dec. 13, 1697.

LETTER VI.

To *James Currie*, Merchant in *Pentland.*

My dear Friend,—I have had a sore fit of my colick since I saw you, and still indisposed ; but O, He does all things well ; and I think, indeed, Christ and His crofs in such a day is no small mercy.   Our light and toom vefsel would soon coup if Christ's ballast were a-wanting, and soon sink if but a little overloaden. Well knows He how to order and steer His crazy and poor ship thro' thir lower seas : what wind we take, what water we draw, and what storms we may bide ; He is our Maker, Pilot, Owner, Merchant, and all Himself : not, indeed, like the world's carpenters, who, when they build their ship, send her to sea, and enquire no more after her.   O ! that we know Him so little, and that He is known no more ; and if known, who would not love, serve, admire, and adore Him.   But alas! this world is crying for want of corn and wine ; neither seeing nor sorrowing for our abominable iniquities ; nor how to avert the present nor approaching vengeance that is following ; nor seeing the glory of His justice that is displaying in the nations as a banner.   O to be found in Him, like Him, and for Him.   No other thing will do it ; silver and gold, barns and garnels, ships and armies, king and counsellors, when all joined together, will not do it.   He will go through them, and break them down as a fire doth thorns. O for a life of faith, a life of diligence and on-waiting ; for He is

surely on His way. Now my respects to yourself, kind bed-
fellow, and family. Your mercies are not few : the Lord help
you to improve them to His glory. Now Himself be with you
all.—I am, dear Friend, *yours affectionately,*   R. HAMILTON.

Borrowftounnefs, Nov. 33, 1698.

LETTER VII.

To *James Currie,* Merchant in *Pentland.*

Dear and Chriftian Friend,—The case and trials of your family
came not to my hand till this day. I long to hear how it is with
you. I hope He is letting you see the need of all, and making
you say—*It is the Lord, let Him do whatsoever He will* with me
and mine. He is a wise Manager ; it is His hand that can do no
wrong ; a skilful, tender, and loving Physician that knows how
to mix his potions to the best advantage. O let us *commit our
way to Him,* and *trust in Him,* and *cast our care on Him ; for
He careth for us.* His defign is but to melt off our drofs, and
draw us near Himself. O to be living under lively impreffions of
our interest in and relation to that glory that is above, and of
that infinite love that has purchased and procured it to us ; how
would it encourage us to mend our pace homeward, and to bear
patiently all blasts and storms in the way ; thro' them we must,
but if once there, how happy were we. O to be lifting up our
eyes and seeing, and then lifting up our heads and rejoicing, to
see how by every duty and difficulty our redemption draweth
nigh. If our eyes were more heavenward and homeward, there
would be lefs fretting and wearying in our way. O, brother, what
is here to detain holy souls ? *Zion* is made a desolation, truth
murdered, holinefs mocked, the godly despised, wickednefs and
all defection abounding, graces withering, and love decaying ;

but ah! the cup is going round : it is in *the hand of the Lord, and the wine is red : it is full of mixture, and He poureth out the same; but the dregs thereof all the wicked of the earth shall wring them out and drink them*—*Psalm* lxxv. 8. But I will not detain you. My love to your kind bed-fellow, self, and family. The Lord be with you all.—I am, dear Friend, *yours &c.*,   R. HAMILTON.

Sept. 4, 1699.

LETTER VIII.

To *James Currie*, Merchant in *Pentland*, after the whole Family had the Fever.

Chriſtian and dear Friend,—At my coming here I was much refreshed to hear that the Lord had so mercifully dealt with your family, in bringing you all safely thro' such boisterous storms, when so many, in all airths, of greater bulk and strength, are sunk and split. The Lord Himself make us to improve and employ our mercies singly for Him. He is doing great things, and will perfect His work, tho' we neither know when nor how. I was comforting myself to have seen you at this place, otherways neither my ease nor convenience would have stopt me to have seen you at the *Ferry;* however, I was glad ye did take it so well; for, indeed, I think it should be all our businefs to keep up these despised meetings, should it be but for a witnefs of what has been, and yet is, and may be ; and to see one another, whom this generation cares not for seeing of. However, I hope to see you at the next tryst, tho' my health still remains very uncertain ; yet bleffings to Him that debates in measure. Now tho' I have but little to say, yet I cannot be silent when I have occafion.

My love and respects to yourself and kind family, referring all till meeting.—I am *your afsured Friend,*   R. HAMILTON.

Borrowftounnefs, Nov. 11, 1699.

LETTER IX.

To *James Currie*, Merchant in *Pentland*.

My dear Friend,—Could my sympathy at this time be steadable to you, I may say He knows you want it not. God has more shown His will, ye are to show your obedience, submission, and complacency in it. He allows your being concerned and affected with your trial ; but here is superabounding comfort, that He not only allows Himself to sympathize with you in it, but to be *afflicted in all your afflictions*, and withal has given you a signal door of hope, not *to mourn as those that are without hope*, but to rejoice in His eternal love that ever condescended and ordained out of your loins a twig of glory ; and ascribe glory to Him who, as He has promised *to be better than ten sons to you*, so, as an incomparable Father, has taken home His own child to an uninterrupted communion with Himself, out of the world, from the imminent snares and dangers thereof, to these chambers and mansions of glory, safety and ease, rest and security, when *he shall say no more he is sick* or pained, out of the dint of all storms, fears, and tentations. O, brother, the days are coming when such a trial will not only be thought easy, but pure and matchless mercy. But my scribblings, I judge, will but trouble you to read them ; it is He that has given the wound must apply the plaister to you all. Well can He do it, and I hope He will do it. The Lord Himself be with you all. O my heart bleeds on all your behalfs. The Lord Himself step in amongst you ; a word from Himself will do, and will comfort your afflicted souls, and put off the tempter, who at such a time is not idle. I could have no rest till I sent out *William*. The Lord's blessing and mine to yourself and afflicted bed-fellow and family.— *Yours, in all duty,*   R. Hamilton.

Letters from Mr. James Kid.*

To *Helen Alexander*, Spouse to *James Currie*, upon the death of
her Son, *Thomas Currie*.

Borrowſtounneſs, March 14, 1698.

Chriſtian Friend,—Though I be very unfit to write anything to
you as your present circumſtances require, all that I can say being
only words very taſteleſs to an afflicted soul, yet I could not slip
the occaſion of letting you know that I desire not to be altogether
unmindfull of you, otherwise I shᵈ be very far from the duty of
sympathy, wʰ. Religion binds upon all its Profeſsours, though I
had no particular delegations to your family beyond many others
for your undeserved kindness to me since I had any acquaintance
with you.   I know it is the Lord alone who hath given you the
ſtroak, & He only can bind up & speak comfort to purpose ; &
I believe the more you are eying Him in it, ye shall have the
more peace afterward, when you shall see there was a neceſſity
for this as well as for all the other ſteps of His providence, who

* Mr. JAMES KID, of Borrowſtounneſs, was collector and treasurer for the
general meetings of the Societies.   About 1691 he appears to have been a
ſtudent of theology at Utrecht, where he suffered imprisonment.   In 1699 the
Societies resolved to send Mr. Kid and Mr. Charles Umpherſton to Holland
for licence and ordination, but this was not accompliſhed.   See APPENDIX,
Note B,—*Dr. Charles Umpherſton*.   Mr. Kid left the Societies in 1704, and
joined the Church of Scotland.

doth all things well, & can do no wrong ; & whatever harſh thoughts we may have of His way of dealing with us, yet none of us can make straight what many of us are too ready to think He hath made crooked. It is true I have never had the experience of loſs of children, & therefore must be excused if I speak of that kind of afflicĉtion as maiden midwives speak to women in childbirth, yet I know that Death, by snatching away a hopefull son, cannot but take a cruel grip of the bowels of a tender-hearted mother. I believe, likewise, the Lord is this day observing your carriage under His hand when He is (as it were) burying a piece of you under the earth. Therefore, I wᵈ think it beſt for you to let Him do with His own what He will. He found us at nothing in our beginning, & tho' He shᵈ bring us to nothing again what unjuſtice shᵈ He do us ? If the Lord hath seen anything in you or your family that nothing leſs cᵈ help than the death of a dear son, I wish the Lord Himself may bleſs the Dispensation. However, mourn not as those without hope ; remember Sathan loves to fish in troubled waters, & finds too much room for his tempta.ⁿˢ even in the troubled souls of the Lord's deareſt people. Charge your soul to be quiet, & to adore Him who cᵈ as easily have taken your husband, & all the reſt of your children as that one ; & yet it had even then been your duty to have said— *The Lord hath given & the Lord hath taken, bleſsed be His name : all His paths are mercy and truth ; & I know, O Lord, that Thy judgments are right, & that in faithfulneſs Thou haſt afflicted me.* Labour to make a Chriſtian use of the present tryal, you shall be the better in case to bear the next, wᵏ may have more bitter ingredients in it. I cease to trouble you further. The Lord Himself comfort you. So, with my love to you & all the family,— *I am your aſsured Friend & soul's well-wiſher,*

JAMES KID.

To *Helen Alexander*, Spouse to *James Currie*, upon the death of their oldest Son, *James Currie*.

Borrowſtounneſs, March 5, 1701.

Chriſtian & dear Friend,—I have been too long from writing you, but every day expecting a line from your son made me delay. I nothing doubt but it will be work enough for you to get your thoughts set off the loſs of your sweet son, & to subject your affections to His holy will who doth all well. Yet you are not ignorant that, as Sathan is busy with the beſt at such times, so you shᵈ not be idle left discontented thoughts arise in your heart. You know it is your duty at all times, & especially now under the tryall, to advance faith by living above the world even while you are in it; & faith gives the soul allways another fight of the crofs than sense or natural affection doth. Again, labouring for afsurance of His love, & trying the clearnefs of our intereſt in Himself as our soul's portion, is another piece of work wherewith we ought to be exercised. But if the Lord take your son a while out of your fight, you muſt neither judge of love nor hatred by that, for it is no sure mark : alike events happen to all. We must labour to get our hearts humbled for fin, & our consciences cleansed by the blood of JESUS, who (no doubt) wᵈ have us taught by the crofs to deny ourselves & mortify our desires to time's things, & also to moderate our delights in them when we have them ; and thereby we shall the more contentedly part with them when Infinite Wisdom sees fit to pull them from us. Children are God's heritage ; yet He who gives may take, & none of His creatures fhould challenge Him for it, far less they who have given up their souls & bodies & all that belongs to them to His fatherly disposal. You know He might have made you barren, or never have given you a desirable sight of the fruit of your womb ; therefore, blefs His name for what He hath done either to you or yours. He never sent you a dinner nor a drink of water, but He observed your carriage how you w.^d improve it either for His glory, or your own soul's advantage, far lefs hath He sent such a fharp rod as the burying a piece of your flesh without looking for some fruits. But oh, alas! our barrennefs may fhame us. His wisdom & our folly are much to be seen in all His ways towards us, & ours towards Him. But the more of heaven that is in us, the lefs measure of temporal comforts will content us. You know how His Providences are represented by the speckled horses among the myrtle-trees,—*Zachariah* i. 8. God doth speckle His work by interweaving mercies with afflictions. You want a son that once you had, but you have (as yet) a husband that once you wanted. You want one good thing, but you have a better : you have one ill thing, but you want a worse. Therefore, be content to have some of the evils of sorrow about you, while you have so many of the evils of sin within you. We are not compleatly sanctifyed in this life, and we are but fools if we think to be fully satisfyed ; for, when we come to a state of perfect holinefs, it is soon enough to enjoy perfect happinefs.

Remember me to your husband and all the family, and cause *Mr. Charles* write more frequently to let me know how you are. My service to your daughter, & tell her I acknowledge myself her debtor for my night-cap, w.^h I received, with a comb. The Lord be with you, and sanctify the afflicting dispensa.ⁿ wherewith He hath been and is exercising your family, w.^h is the desire of *your real tho' worthless Friend*, JAMES KID.

Letter from Mr. John McMillan* to James Currie, Merchand, upon the death of his dear Wife.

Eastforth, 29th March, 1729.

Dear Brother,—You had never till now an occafion of writing letters upon such a melancholy subject as the death of your godly but now glorified once Spouse. But now she is no more yours but her Lord's, who loved her & gave Himself for her. Now she fings, but you figh; she rejoiceth, but you mourn, w^h sh^d not be so much for her lofs as envying her poft and place; for her tears are wiped off her cheeks, but yours may yet trickle down; sorrow & sighing have left her, but yours for a time may continue. But it's comfortable that it's only in the world that His people hath tribulation. Tho' ye knew the time of meeting when you came together in the relation of husband & wife, you could not tell when the time of parting might be, or on whose fide Death sh^d firft lowse the relation. But now you can tell & say that she is gone

---

* The Rev. JOHN McMILLAN (1669-1753) was minifter of the parifh of Balmaghie, but was deposed by the Presbytery of Kirkcudbright in 1706, on the sole ground of his refusal to retract a paper which he had presented to the Presbytery, craving redress of grievances, and advocating Cameronian principles. In 1706, he joined the United Societies, and became their first minister. His son, the Rev. John McMillan, married Elizabeth, daughter of Dr. Charles Umpherfton.—See APPENDIX, Note B,—*Rev. John McMillan.*

before you, & entered Heir to the matchlefs Inheritance that's uncorruptible & fadeth not away. If we c^d lay to our ears & liften to what the glorified cry to all below, it w^d be thus :—*O prepare and make ready, for with us we have allways a summer without a winter; allways our sun fhines without an intervening cloud; with us is all day but no night,—no mortality in this country; for the inhabitants say not they are fick, & the people that dwelleth there are forgiven their iniquity; with us is the tree of life w^h yieldeth fruit every month, so that the inhabitants have a continual feast, & yet their fomachs never cloaged.* Tho' the Lord hath taken from you the wife of your youth & old age, yet quarrell not. Your loan hath been long be many others. The Lord hath said it that all things shall work together for good to His own. It's the Lord who can make up such lofses, and support & comfort under such crofses. The Lord, by taking away His own in every place, seems to say that He is hafting on His work of judgment on this finfull nation.

I hope the Lord will give you good out of your present dispensation, & sanctify the same to you, which shall be the desire of, *dear Brother, your sympathizing Brother,*

JOHN McMILLAN.

My wife sympathizeth with you, & hath her love kindly remembered to you all. Remember me to all of you as named. I received yours & Mr. CHARLES' letters this day, and have not time to write to JAMES.

Inscription on the Martyrs' Monument Greyfriars' Churchyard, Edinburgh.

Halt paffenger, take heed what you do fee,
This tomb doth fhew, for what fome men did die.

Here lies interr'd the duft of thofe who ftood
'Gainft perjury, refifting unto blood ;
Adhering to the Covenants, and laws
Eftablifhing the fame ; which was the caufe
Their lives were facrificed unto the luft
Of Prelatifts abjur'd.   Though here their duft
Lies mixt with murderers, and other crew,
Whom juftice juftly did to death purfue ;
But as for them, no caufe was to be found
Worthy of death, but only they were found,
Conftant and ftedfaft, zealous, witneffing
For the Prerogatives of CHRIST their KING.
Which Truths were feal'd by famous Guthrie's head,
And all along to Mr. Renwick's blood.
They did endure the wrath of enemies,
Reproaches, torments, deaths, and injuries.
But yet they're thofe who from fuch troubles came,
And now triumph in glory with the LAMB.

From May 27th, 1661, that the moſt noble Marquis of Argyle was beheaded, to the 17th of Febʳʸ, 1688, that Mr. James Renwick ſuffered; were one way or other Murdered and Deſtroyed for the ſame Cauſe, about Eighteen thouſand, of whom were execute at *Edinburgh* about an hundred of Noblemen, Gentlemen, Miniſters and Others; noble Martyrs for JESUS CHRIST. The moſt of them lie here.

For a particular account of the cauſe, and manner of their Suffering, *see* the Cloud of Witneſſes, Crookſhank's and Defoe's Hiſtories.

Rev. vi. 9, 10, 11.
And when he had opened the fifth seal, I saw under the altar the souls of them that were slain for the word of God, and for the Testimony which they held. And they cried with a loud voice, saying, How long, O Lord, holy and true, dost thou not judge and avenge our blood on them that dwell on the earth? And white robes were given to every one of them, and it was said unto them, that they should rest yet for a little season, until their fellow-servants also, and their brethren that should be killed as they *were*, should be fulfilled.

Rev. vii. 14. These are they which came out of great tribulation, and have washed their robes, and made them white in the blood of the Lamb. Chapᵣ 2ᵈ 10. Be thou faithfull unto death, and I will give thee a crown of life.

This Tomb was firſt Erected by James Currie, Merchᵗ in Pentland, and others, 1706. Renewed 1771.

DESCENDANTS OF CHARLES UMPHERSTON

	Children.	Grand-Children.	Gt. Grand-Children.
	Dr. Chas. Umpherston 1678–1758 *Elizabeth Steele* 16—–1743	Eliz. Umpherston 1728–65 *Rev. John M'Millan* 1729–1808 John Umpherston 1723–48	Rev. John M'Millan } *Mary Newton* } Dr. Chas. M'Millan Josias M'Millan Elizabeth M'Millan Alexander M'Millan Andrew M'Millan
			James Umpherston John Umpherston Marg. Umpherston } *James Nicolson* } Marion Umpherston Anable Umpherston } *Robert Paterson* } Eliz. Umpherston } 1750–1812 } *Robert Lang* }
Chas. Umpherston } 16—–1681 } Helen Alexander } 1654–1729 }	James Umpherston 1676–1756 *Marion Brown* 1671–1759	James Umpherston 1709–30 Chas. Umpherston } 1714 — } Helen M'Neil } 1715 — } *(See below, A.)* Anabel Umpherston Helen Umpherston *(See below, B.)*	Chas. Umpherston } 1756–1842 } *Elizabeth Oliphant* } 1770–1835 }
			Beatrix Umpherston } 1743–1823 } *George Carmichael* }
	Beatrix Umpherston 1673–1763 *Rev. John M'Neil,* 1666–1732	James M'Neil 1712–48 *Margaret Stoddart* William M'Neil Helen Umpherston *(See above, B.)* Janet M'Neil *Robert Hutchison* Helen M'Neil *(See above, A.)*	}—John M'Neill }—The Hutchisons —

Inscriptions on Tombstones in the Family Burying-Ground, Pentland.

—◦◦◦—

This is the burial place
apointed for JAMES CURRIE
Marchant in PENTLAND and his
Spoufe HELEN ALLEXANDER of whom
Here refts the corps of JAMES
CURRIE who died . Jan : 19 AO, 1701
his age, 13 years. THOMAS CURRIE
died Feb : 21 AO, 1698, his age
8 years & WILLIAM CURRIE
died Feb : 5th AO, 1694 ; his age
was one year & ROBERT
CURRIE who died June
27th AO, 1706 & of his Age
the   11th   year.

———

JAMES CURRIE
died March 24
An : 1736 Ag'd 80

HELEN ALEXANDER
died March 10
An : 1729 Ag'd 75

(NOTE.—*The above is on the edges of the ftone.*)

JAMES   (EPITAPH)   CURRIE

Stay, Paſsenger, a word or two with thee.
Death ſtrikes the young as well as old we see.
His reliques here ly in this dormitory
Whose ſoul we truſt now ſings his maker's glory.
This hope doth make his friends from grief refrain
That ſoul and body ſhall unite again
No more to ſin no more to ſigh or dy
But live and ſing GOD'S praiſe
          ETERNALLY.

(NOTE.—*The above is on the back of the ſtone.*)

HERE LIES

CHARLES UMPHERSTON
Tenant in PENTLAND
who died Decʳ 1681.
Vivit Poſt Funera Virtus.

Alſo his Son JAMES
UMPHERSTON Merchᵗ there
who died Febʳ 12ᵗʰ 1756,
in the 80ᵗʰ year of his Age
And his Spouſe MARION
BROWN who died Febʳ 4
1759, in the 88ᵗʰ year of her
Age. Likewise their son
JAMES UMPHERSTON who
died Septʳ 26ᵗʰ 1730 in the
21ˢᵗ year of his age. And
two of their son CHARLES'S
Children who died in their Infancy.

K

HERE LYS

The dust of Mr John
McNeil Preacher of the
Gospel at Loanhead ; who
died 10ᵗʰ Decʳ 1732, in the
66ᵗʰ year of his age.
A faithful adherent to the
Covenanted Teſtimony of the
Church of Scotland in Principle
& Practice and a conſtant Witnefs
againſt Defection from said
Teſtimony. Alfo the duſt
of Beatrix Umpherston his
Spoufe who died Febʳ 27ᵗʰ 1763
in the 90ᵗʰ year of her Age.
And of James McNeil their
son who died Novʳ 24ᵗʰ 1748 in the
36ᵗʰ year of his age.

———•———

Hic jacet Doctor doctus in Duplice arte
Curandi corpus et eruditus meliori parte
Nec divitus nec dolibus in ultº tempore elatus
Sed cœla sanctorum putavit se esse beatum.

Here rests the Dust of Mr. Charles Umpher-
stone, Surgeon in Pentland, an ornament to Society, Learning & Piety in Life, & a Stedfast witnefs

for the Cov:ᵈ Presb:ⁿ Reformation to the last, who
died 21ˢᵗ Jan:ʸ 1758 & 80:ᵗʰ year of his age.
Alſo ELISABETH STEEL his wife who died 9:ᵗʰ Sep:ʳ
1743, His son JOHN UMPHERSTON who
died much Lamented Dec:ʳ 10. 1748 Aged 25
years, And his D:ʳ ELIZABETH UMPHER-
STONE born 31ˢᵗ Jan:ʸ 1728, Married to yᵉ Revᵈ M:ʳ
JOHN MCMILLAN 27:ᵗʰ Dec:ʳ 1749 & after 5 years
fore affliction died 24:ᵗʰ Feb:ʸ 1765 leaving a
Husband & 6 children to lament yᵉ loſs of a
Pious Loving wife and mother.

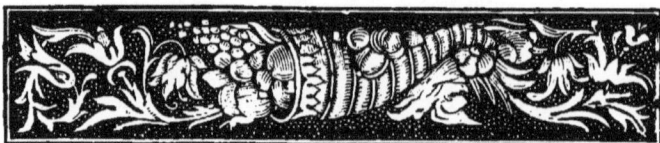

APPENDIX.

Note A.—The Children's Covenant. (See Page 12).

THE following is taken from a volume in the possession of the Rev. Josias A. Chancellor, Belfast, entitled "A Collection of Dying Testimonies of some Holy and Pious Christians who lived in Scotland before and since the Revolution, &c., &c.; also the various ways of the Lord's Providential Dealings with some of them; with several of their Personal Covenantings."—*Kilmarnock*, 1806. The first name appended to the Covenant is that of Beatrix Umpherston, daughter of Helen Alexander. At the date of the Covenant, 1683, Beatrix Umpherston was a child of 10 years of age. She became the wife of the Rev. John McNeil. See Table of the Descendants of Charles Umpherston and Helen Alexander.

A Covenant Transaction with the LORD, *by a Society of young Children, who met together in a meeting at* PENTLAND *Town, in the time of Persecution, when there was no faithful Minister in* SCOTLAND, *anno* 1683, *ere that great burning and shining light,* Mr. JAMES RENWICK, *came an ordained Minister from* HOLLAND.

THIS is a Covenant made between the LORD and us, with our whole hearts, and to give up ourselves freely to Him, without reserve, soul and body, hearts and affections, to be His children, and Him to be our GOD and FATHER, if it please the holy Lord to send His Gospel to the land again. That we stand to this Covenant which we have written between the LORD and us, as we shall answer at the great day ; that we shall never break this Covenant which we have made between the LORD and us. That we shall stand to this Covenant which we have made ; and if not, it shall be a witness against us in the great day, when we shall stand before the LORD and His holy angels. O, Lord, give us real grace in our hearts to mind *Zion's* breaches, that is in such a low case this day ; and make us to mourn with her, for Thou hast said, *them that mourn with her in the time of her trouble, shall rejoice when she rejoiceth ; when the Lord will come and bring back the captivity of Zion*, when He shall deliver her out of her enemies' hands ; when her King shall come and raise her from the dust, in spite of all her enemies that will oppose her, either devils or men. Tho' thus they have banished her King *Christ* out of the land, yet He will arise and avenge His children's blood at her enemies' hands, which cruel murderers have shed.

[*Upon the back of this Covenant was written as follows :—*]

Them that will not stand to every article of this Covenant, which we have made betwixt the LORD and us, that they shall not go to the *Kirk* to hear any of these soul-murdering Curates, we will neither speak nor converse with them. Any that breaks this Covenant they shall never come into our society. We shall declare before the LORD, that we have bound ourselves in Covenant, to be covenanted to Him all the days of our life, to be His children and Him our covenanted Father.

We subscribe with our hands these presents :—

BEATRIX UMPHERSTON.	MARGARET BROWN.
JANET BROWN.	JANET BROWN.
HELEN MOUTRAY.	ISOBEL CRAIG.
MARION SWAN.	MARTHA LOGAN.
JANET SWAN.	AGNES AITKIN.
MARGARET GALLOWAY.	MARIAN McMOREN.
HELEN STRAITON.	CHRISTIAN LAURIE.
HELEN CLARK.	

B.—Notes to the Table of Helen Alexander's Descendants.

I.—Dr. Charles Umpherston (1678-1758).

The Rev. Josias A. Chancellor, of Belfast, has kindly supplied the following extracts and observations from a MS. copy of the " Register of the General Meetings of the old Dissenters," which is in his possession :—

" A meeting, held at Crawford John, October 25, 1699, to see if any would go abroad to be licensed and ordained. They wished to send four at that time to Holland. They had two in their eye to go abroad, Mr. James Kid and Mr. Charles Umpherston. Sir Robert Hamilton was to go to Holland before them, but was now gravelish through imprisonment, and unable ; so it came to nothing."

April 5, 1704. The General Meeting having received a letter from the Rev. John McMillan requesting a conference with them, Mr. Charles Umpherston, and six other brethren, were appointed to confer with Mr. McMillan. This appointment was renewed the following year.

July 11, 1705. A committee was appointed "to draw up a vindication of our Public Testimonies since the Revolution, with Scriptural Probation, approven Divines, and Records of Parliaments and Assemblies." Mr. Charles Umpherston and a few others were chosen for this work ; and the different correspondences were directed to send to Pentland an account of their several contendings for the preservation of the Testimony.

August 6, 1707. The General Meeting resolved to draw up a protestation against the Union of Scotland and England then effected. At the next meeting various drafts were presented and considered. That by Mr. Charles Umpherston was found the fullest and fittest, and was chosen for publication.

August 7, 1727. Messrs. John McNeil, Charles Umpherston, &c., were appointed to give a short answer to "Carnwath's and Carsland's Memoirs, together with Patrick Walker's Scandallous Pamphlets," &c.

August 3, 1733. Messrs. McMain, Charles Umpherston, Gilbert Melvil, and James Umpherston were appointed to prepare a draft of the steps of defection from the covenanted work of Reformation by both Church and State, to be laid before the four Associate Ministers, Messrs. Ebenezer Erskine, Wilson, Moncrieff, and Fisher.

Nov. 21, 1733. "There came a letter from our worthy friend, James Currie, in Pentland, concerning the publishing the Dying Testimony of Sir Robert

Hamilton, with his other public papers relating to the Testimony. The General Meeting desire the foresaid James Currie to give three papers he hath by him to Mr. McMain's and Mr. Charles Umpherston's hand, that they may revise and make remarks on them against the next meeting in order to publishing."

March 4, 1734. "The General Meeting, being constitute by prayer by the Rev. John McMillan, Mr. Charles Umpherston was chosen preses. The General Meeting, having got a full account of the Committee's diligence with the four [Associate] Ministers at Dumfermline, did unanimously approve of the whole thereof, and also did appoint Mr. Charles Umpherston to attend Messrs. Ebenezer Erskine and Moncrieff at Edinburgh the second Wednesday of this instant, farther to converse with them, and to show our sympathy and concern with them."

Oct. 28, 1734. "The General Meeting, having considered the whole of that affair of the four [Associate] Brethren, thought it expedient to appoint Mr. Charles Umpherston and Mr. John McMain, &c., to draw up a paper against the next meeting, showing the difference and inconsistency between their Public Testimony and our last Conference with them at Dumfermline, and the reasons why we cannot join with them.

"Applications were made by the several Correspondences to have fit persons to visit and examine Fellowships; whereupon the Rev. Mr. McMillan, the elders, and the General Meeting do appoint and commissionate Mr. John McMain, Mr. Charles Umpherston, and Mr. Alexander Marshall to go through and visit the Societies, and in their examination to be agreeable to the Scriptures, our Confession of Faith, and Catechisms."

May 30, 1737. "Mr. Charles Umpherston was appointed preses of the meeting. The General Meeting, taking into consideration that important affair of the succession of a Gospel Ministry, the means used hitherto proving ineffectual, our destitute and extraordinary case still continuing, not knowing how soon we may be deprived of the light we yet enjoy, give it as their unanimous mind that our reverend pastor call forth to the office of the holy ministry Messrs. Charles Umpherston and Alexander Marshall, whom we judge the most fit and qualified among us, being already teaching elders, and of known integrity."

Mr. Charles Umpherston was the principal compiler of the Testimony which was published at Mount Herick, near Crawford John, May 7th, 1741, and termed the *Mount Herick Testimony*, an able document, now rarely to be met with.

The first Reformed Presbytery met at Braehead, August 1st, 1743, and was constituted of the Rev. Messrs. John McMillan and Thomas Nairn, ministers of the Gospel, and Mr. Charles Umpherston and William Vetch, ruling elders.

II.—JAMES UMPHERSTON (1676-1756).

A Paper wrote by JAMES UMPHERSTON *a few months before his death.*

(From the original in the possession of Francis Umpherston, Esq.)

I am looking every day for my dissolution ; but I can say but little, for I have been and am guiltie of many sins, and have not improven my time as I sh^d have done, which is matter of my sorrow and lamentation. Notwithstanding of the many favours and mercies I have been priviledged with, I have not improven them ; and now I am well stricken in years, but what have I done for the advantage of His glory in my days ? I am a poor useless creature, and can do little service ; but I desire to leave my testimony to all the truths contained in the Holy Scriptures, and the testimony that the poor remnant have been adhering to, and I desire to believe it's their honour so to do, and will be, if they continue steadfast to the cause of CHRIST, whatever their imperfections have been ; and I desire to believe that the Lord will yet arise and plead His own cause, in spite of all opposition, when His set time comes to favour His *Zion*. But as for myself I am a poor unsignificant creature, and can do service so as I may be well wanted ; but I desire to bless the Lord that ever I heard the Gospel preached by *Mr. McMillan* and others. But, alas! I have not walked agreeable thereto (w^h I desire to lament before the Lord), notwithstanding His kindness to me in bestowing many mercies upon me after I have broken my vows unto Him, w^h I made more than fifty years since in covenanting away myself to Him, and also several times, and wherein I failed and came short. I was sore casten down. Several Scriptures came into my mind, and that in *Heb.* viii. 12 :—*I will be merciful to thy unrighteousness, and thy sins and iniquities I will remember no more :* and many others, as *Isaiah* xlii. 2 ; *Psalms* xxv. 11 ; w^h gave me some comfort through the Lord's word. But what shall I say to the Lord's commendation ? I cannot commend Him enough for His free love and undeserved favour to me and mine. It was my earnest desire to the Lord that, if ever He was pleased to change my state to a married, He might direct my way in that. So it was His holy will to tryst me with a godly wife, w^h was a great blessing, w^h I have reason to bless the Lord that ever I was trysted so. She was both a wife and a parent to me to instruct and teach both me and my children, and gave many good advices to me and them. And now, I leave them all upon the Lord to direct them through all the snares and tentations that may come in their way, and carry them safe through.   JAMES UMPHERSTON.

Pentland, Nov.ᵗ 14ᵗʰ 1755.

III.—Rev. JOHN McNEIL (1666-1732)

Was a licentiate of the Church of Scotland, but was deprived of license by his Presbytery for no other reason than for protesting against certain public actions of the Church, and sympathizing with the views of the Cameronian Covenanters. He joined the Societies in 1707. In September, 1708, a protestation, declinature, and appeal was sent to the General Assembly by Mr. McMillan and Mr. McNeil, in which they declared their principles, protested that the sentences pronounced by the Church courts were not binding on them, and appealed to the first free, faithful, and rightly-constituted Assembly of the Church. Mr. McNeil's license, dated May 10th, 1699, is in the possession of Francis Umpherston, Esq.

IV.—Rev. JOHN McMILLAN (1729-1808),

Son of Rev. John McMillan of Balmaghie, was ordained at Bothwell in 1750, and was afterwards settled at Pentland. He subsequently became minister at Sandhills, parish of Shettlestone, and, in 1786, accepted the pastoral charge of the Glasgow Reformed Presbyterian Congregation. He died February 11th, 1808, in the 79th year of his age, and 58th of his ministry.

V.—ELIZABETH UMPHERSTON (1728-1765), daughter of Dr. Charles Umpherston, and wife of the above Rev. John McMillan.

The following particulars of the death of Mrs. McMILLAN *are taken from the diary of (James) Brown, in the possession of Christopher Aitchison :—*

On Sabbath evening, February 24th, 1765, died Mrs. McMillan, after about five years' illness of a palsy. Her husband this day was preaching at Hamilton, on *Heb.* xii.:—"See that ye refuse not to hear Him that speaketh from heaven." She expired in the evening 'twixt ten and eleven, and it was Monday morning about ten before he arrived.

The subjoined extract from the same diary, being of some family interest, is also added :—

Neither my indulgent parent [James Brown (1679-1765), brother of Marion

L

Brown, the wife of James Umpherston] nor Mrs. McMillan could speak much for some days before their deaths. My father was born in March, 1679, and near lived out 86. His mother, Anable Cleghorn, about the time of his childhood, was persecuted and hunted for her steadfastness to Covenanted Reformation. His father, James Brown, died soon after my father's birth. His only sister, Marion Brown, died about six years ago, and was much about my father's age when she died. My father was married before he married my mother. He had a son called John to her, who was eminent for religion, and who died about 1738 or '39 at Loanhead, and was buried in Pentland buryingplace, near the spot where my father is laid. He has left behind him of children two daughters, Isb. and Marion, and myself, the youngest, who am against the 16th of May first, if I be spared till that time, entered into my 30th year. My younger sister is married a year past in December last, and has a child named Mary, after my mother, whose name was Mary Scot, born likewise of religious parents. Arthur Taket, who suffered in the Grassmarket, was a relation of her forefathers. I've heard my father frequently tell that Messrs. Cargill, and Smith, and Boig were lodged in his mother's house the night before they were taken, and that Mr. Cargill lectured on the 11th chapter of *Zechariah*, and, when at the 4th and 5th verses, expressed, by way of prophecy, that the time sh^d soon be when there sh^d be no faithful shepherds left to feed the flock of slaughter, which came to pass ; for, from the death of the eminent Mr. J. Renwick till Mr. John M'Millan came off from the present Revolution Church, the poor wasted handfull had no public teacher for 18 years. [*Dated Thursday March 7th*, 1765.]

VI.—ANABEL UMPHERSTON, daughter of James Umpherston and Marion Brown.

A personal Covenant by ANABEL UMPHERSTON.

(From the original in Mr. F. Umpherston's possession).

O most gracious and holy LORD GOD, I, Thy poor unworthy creature, do here most solemnly prostrate myself at the footstool of Thy mercy, humbly beseeching Thee to accept of me for the sake and merits of the dear Son of Thy love, and to pardon my so long delay of this duty of solemn personal covenanting with Thee, although I have often verbally done it ; and I, being convinced from Thy Word, that it is a bound duty not only to say with the mouth, but also to subscribe with the hand, to be the Lord's, and having for a long time had some resolutions to set about the duty, yet still neglecting it, for which and all my other sins both of omission and commission I desire to be humble before Thee.

And now, O LORD, I do renew all my former engagements, and also my baptismal vows wherein I was most solemnly devoted to Thee, to be Thine, and for Thee, and to renounce the devil, the world, and the flesh. And as my parents engaged for me while in infancy, so I do now take them upon myself, humbly begging grace and strength from Thee, to enable me to perform these mine engagements. And I do again solemnly covenant and give myself wholly to Thee, soul and body, to be at Thy disposal; and I do take Thee for my only GOD, Guide, and Portion, and for all that I want for time and for eternity; and I desire with all my heart to bless Thee for that noble device of salvation, and to close w^t it, and to accept of CHRIST on the terms He is offered in the Gospel, to be my Prophet, Priest, and King. And as I am by nature blind and ignorant, I take Him for my Teacher and Leader to guide me in the way of truth and duty in this cloudy and dark day; and being both guilty and filthy by original sin and innumerable actual transgressions, I take Him for my Priest to atone for my guilt, and to make intercession for me. I desire wholly to renounce all mine own righteousness, and to cast it away as rotten rags, and to take Him for my Wisdom, Righteousness, Sanctification, and compleat Redemption; and I do betake myself to His blood alone for washing and cleansing from all these filthy stains that sin hath made upon my soul. And as I have many and strong spiritual enemys to wrestle with, I take Him for my King to subdue and conquere all these my strong lusts and corruptions, desiring humbly and heartily to submit myself to His government.

And now, O LORD, I desire to bless Thee for what Thou hast done for me in that thou hast cast my lot to be in a land of light, and where the Gospel is preached, and that I have had religious education and example; yea, and hast followed me with loving-kindness and tender mercies. And even when I was running away from Thee, and pursuing my lusts, what pains hast Thou taken to reclame and bring me back again, and hast in some measure convinced me of the evil of my ways, of my lost state by nature, and also discovered to me a remedy through CHRIST; and, when sore cast down, hast given me such comfort from the sweet and precious promises of Thy Word, which Thou hast caused me to take for a ground of my sure hope.

And now, holy LORD GOD, as I have entered into a marriage covenant with Thee, and must be divorced from all other lovers, I do here in Thy name solemnly protest against whatever usurps the room in mine affections that Thou should have; earnestly desiring Thee to take my whole love and affections, and let none rival the throne in my heart with Thee. Now, as I have entered into a personal covenant with Thee, so I desire to bind myself to the Nationall and Solemn League and Covenant, whereby I and the whole land is bound to be for the LORD, and in their place and station to endeavour the advancement of religion and reformation, and the extirpation of whatever is contrair to sound doctrine and the power of godliness ; and resolve through Thy strength, if ever Thou call me to suffer for owning these or any of Thy truths, to undergo the greatest of sufferings rather than wrong Thy truth.

Now, LORD, in the sense of my own weakness and inability to keep or perform these my vows, I desire to look and to rely on Thee for strength and furniture for this and all other dutys incumbent upon me in my place and station ; humbly begging from Thee light and direction so to carry and behave myself in every case and circumstance, that I may keep a conscience void of offence, both towards Thee and towards man. And now, O LORD, I call Thee, who is the Searcher of the heart and Tryer of the reins, to witness that upon my deliberate choice I have taken Thee for my only portion, and that it is the unfeigned resolution of my heart (by Thy grace and strength enabling me) to stand to these my solemn vows and engadgements I am now come under to Thee, over the belly of all oppositions, whether from without or from within ; earnestly desiring that what I have done here on earth (tho' in much weakness and imperfection) may be ratifyed in Heaven. In witness whereof, I do subscribe this with my hand, at *Pentland*, the 23ᵈ day of *August*, 1741.

ANABEL UMPHERSTOUN.

VII.—WILLIAM McNEIL, son of the Rev. John McNeil and Beatrix Umpherston.

A personal Covenant by WILLIAM McNEIL.

(From the original in Mr. F. Umpherston's possession).

O great and mercifull LORD GOD, I do hereby confess and acknowledge that I am a lost and undone Sinner, my nature being wholly depraved and corrupted ; that I am laid under the curse in *Adam* thro' the Breach of yᵉ Covenant of Works ; and that I have ruined myself more and more by my actual transgressions innumerable. I am convinced and do also acknowledge that I am utterly unable to help myself, in whole or in part, out of this Gulf of sin and misery into which I am plunged ; and that it is beyond the reach of the whole Creation to help me out of it : so yᵗ I must inevitably perish for ever, if Thine own strong hand do not make help to me. But seeing there is a Covenant of Grace for life and salvation to lost Sinners established between Thee and Thine own SON the LORD JESUS CHRIST, wherein Thou hast promised that Thou wilt be their GOD and they shall be Thy people, to the making of them holy and happy for ever; and y.ᵗ this Covenant is, in CHRIST the Head thereof, offered and exhibited to me in Thy Gospel, and thou callest me into the Fellowship of it in Him,—therefore, upon the warrant of, and in obedience to Thy Command and Call, I, a poor perishing sinner, do take hold of that Covenant for Life and Salvation to me ; believing on the name of CHRIST crucified, the Head thereof, offered and exhibited to me, as the Great High Priest, who, by the sacrifice of Himself, hath made Atonement, payed the Ransom, and brought in an everlasting Righteousness for poor sinners. I credit His Word of Grace to me, and accordingly trust on Him y.ᵗ He with His Righteousness will be mine, and y.ᵗ in and thro' Him God will be my God, and I shall be one of His People, to y.ᵉ making of me holy and happy for ever.

O, my GOD, I do by Thy Grace acquiese in that Covenant as all my Salvation and all my Desire. With my whole heart and soul, the SON incarnate is my only Priest, my Surety, my Intercessor, and my Redeemer, and, in Him, the FATHER my FATHER, the HOLY GHOST my SANCTIFIER, GOD in CHRIST my GOD. I resign myself Soul and body to Him, to be saved by His Blood alone, renouncing all Confidence in mine own Righteousness, Doings, and Sufferings. With my whole Heart and Soul He is my Head and Husband. And I am His only, wholly, and for ever, to live by Him, to Him, and for Him. I take Him for my alone Prophet, Oracle, and Guide, give up myself wholly to Him, and to be taught, guided, and directed in all things by His Word and Spirit, and renounce mine own wisdom and the wisdom of this World. He is, with my whole heart's consent, my alone King and Lord ; and I resign myself wholly, Soul and Body, unto Him, to be rescued by the strength of His mighty hand from Sin, Death, the Devil, and this present evil World, for to serve Him for ever, and to be ruled by the will of His Command as to my Duty, and the will of His Providence as to my Lot. I am, with my whole heart, content (Lord, Thou knowest y.ᵗ I would fain be at it) to part with, and do renounce every known Sin, Lust, or Idol, and particularly the Sin or Sins which most easily beset me ; together with my own foolish Will, and all other Lords besides Him, without Reservation, and without Exception, against His Cross. Protesting in Thy Sight, O LORD, that I am thro' Grace, willing to have discovered unto me, and upon Discovery to part with, every Sin in me that I know not ; and that the Doubtings and Averseness of heart mixed with this my accepting of Thy Covenant, are what I allow not ; and that notwithstanding thereof, I look to be accepted of Thee herein, in the Beloved, Thine only Son, and my Saviour, purging away these, with all my other Sins, by His precious Blood. Let it be recorded in Heaven, O Lord, and let the stones and timber, and whatever is here present, bear witness that I, tho' most unworthy, have this Day here taken hold of and come into Thy Covenant of Grace, offered and exhibited unto me in Thy Gospel. And that Thou art my God in the Tenor of y^t Covenant, and I am one of Thy people, from henceforth and for ever, I subscribe, with my hand,

WILLIAM McNEIL.

Brachcad, June 24, 1742.

SUPPLEMENTARY NOTE.

JOHN GIB AND HIS SECT.

SEE PAGES 8 AND 28.

JOHN GIB, shipmaster, Borrowstounness, called from his size "Meikle John Gib," was the founder of a small sect, called "Sweet Singers." His followers were so named because they were frequently engaged in singing the penitential Psalms. In April, 1681, Gib, with three men and twenty-six women, retired to the hills to be safe from the dreadful ruin which they believed to be impending on the land. The Gibbites renounced all authority, civil and ecclesiastical, condemned the names of the months and days, and burned the Bible because of its dedication to King James. They were all imprisoned in 1681, but were soon afterwards released. After a short time they were again apprehended, and placed in the Canongate Tolbooth, where "they took such fits of fasting that their voices changed like to the howling of dogs. Gib became so possessed of a roaring devil, like another demoniac, that the sufferers could not get exercise made in the room, which made two of them by turns lie upon him that time, holding a napkin to his mouth." After a severe beating by one George Jackson, he was more easily managed ; and, when religious exercises began, "he would run behind the door, and, with the napkin on his mouth, sit howling like a dog." In 1684 Gib was banished to the Plantations. He died in 1720.

PRINTED BY
MARCUS WARD & CO.,
BELFAST.

www.ingramcontent.com/pod-product-compliance
Lightning Source LLC
Chambersburg PA
CBHW021423090426
42742CB00009B/1231